Baptist Heritage Course

Part 1: The Ancient Church
Scope: First 15 Centuries

Evangelist Ted Alexander, D.D.

HOME STUDY EDITION

Baptist Heritage Course

Part 1: The Ancient Church
Scope: First 15 Centuries

Evangelist Ted Alexander, D.D.

Copyright © 2009 Ted Alexander. All rights reserved.

Writings contained herein are by the author unless otherwise stated.

No part of this publication may be reproduced, stored in a retrieval system or transmitted in any way by any means – electronic, mechanical, photocopy, recording or otherwise – without the prior permission of the copyright holder, except as provided by USA copyright law.

All Scriptures are taken from the King James Bible.

ISBN# 978-1-935075-82-0

Printed in the United States of America.

Printed by Calvary Publishing
A Ministry of Parker Memorial Baptist Church
1902 East Cavanaugh Road
Lansing, Michigan 48910
www.CalvaryPublishing.org

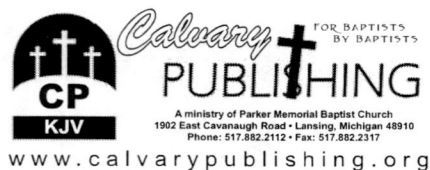

Contents

Lesson One 7
   The Biblical Basis for the Study of Baptist History

Lesson Two 15
   The Problem with Ignorance: How It Happened and What It Has Produced

Lesson Three 25
   The Baptist Beginning: Contrasted with Both Catholic and Protestant Origins

Lesson Four 35
   The Waldenses: Successors to the Apostles

Lesson Five 47
   The Novatians, Montanists

Lesson Six 59
   The Donatists, Paulicians

Lesson Seven 71
   The Albigenses

Lesson Eight 83
The Bogomils, Paterines, Henricians

Lesson Nine 93
The Petrobrussians, Arnoldists

Lesson Ten 103
The Picards, Lollards, Reformation Part I

Lesson Eleven 117
The Reformation Part II, Anabaptists Part I

Lesson Twelve 131
The Anabaptists Part II

Answer Keys 147

Lesson One

Biblical Basis for the Study of Baptist History

> We have heard with our ears, O God, our fathers have told us, *what* work thou didst in their days, in the times of old.
>
> **Psalm 44:1**

The study of our Baptist heritage is a journey into a world of excitement. It leads us backward on a road where we meet many great heroes of the Baptist faith. On this road, we are introduced to the true freedom fighters. We see men and women who seemed to give the whole of their existence in surrender to God, so that subsequent generations could worship the Lord Jesus Christ in full liberty of conscience. We discover stories of real men and women who worked tirelessly to further the Gospel and the Baptist faith. As we continue on this road, it does not take us long to see something else appear; it is the road itself. As we look at it more closely we see that it is covered with blood! This blood is not the blood that we usually think of as Baptist believers, that being the blood of our Lord, rather it is the blood of millions of Baptist martyrs. The boldest of the bold and the bravest of the brave walked here. This is where they lived. This is where they worshipped. This is where they raised their families, and this is where they died. As we examine this trail, we must agree it is truly a "trail of blood." It is a hallowed road where character abounded, faith was multiplied, and God was glorified in the most sacrificial way possible. The things we see here and what they do to our hearts can never be felt and learned if we do not walk the trail.

Sadly, today there is a great disinterest in studying our Baptist heritage. Some question whether it is important or just a waste of time. Many fail to see the relevance for today. This misunderstanding has caused us great damage.

The purpose of lesson one is to lay out the Biblical grounds for studying Baptist history. We will also note the reasons it is so important to both study our heritage and then share it with our children.

The Bible Promotes the Study of Baptist History

Look up and discuss all Scriptures referenced below:

Joshua 1:1-5 In this text, Israel is ready to cross the Jordan River and enter the promised land. This is a huge event in the history of Israel. God is fulfilling a promise he made to Abraham a long time ago. This

LESSON ONE 9

was a long-awaited event. It was the biggest thing to happen to Israel up to this time in history. Our next Scripture reveals to us that God never wanted the Jews to forget this piece of history.

Joshua 4:1-9 God commanded the Jews to set up twelve stones in the Jordan River on this big day.
(A) These stones were set up to teach the generations to come about their heritage. God did not want the future generations to forget how God worked in the past in the lives of their forefathers.
(B) Our generation seems to have forgotten its own history.

Joshua 24:26-27 This text displays another of the many Bible examples of stones of remembrance.
The Word of God clearly teaches that without looking back to past memorials, God's people could easily deny Him.

2 Peter 1:12-13 Peter taught that remembrance was a key to staying stirred up.
(A) Learning of the millions of bleeding, suffering martyrs will stir you up to live for God.
(B) This could be vitally important to our gen-

eration in light of the possibility of coming persecution.

The Book of Acts is a perfect example of God's interest in our knowing Baptist history. Acts is a running history of the early churches.

Hebrews 11 is yet another proof of God's interest in His people knowing their history.

Other Scriptures that endorse studying our history are as follows: **Psalm 90:1-2, Psalm 44:1-3, Psalm 78:1-6, Jeremiah 6:16, Jeremiah 18:15-17, and Deuteronomy 32:7.**

To be sure, the Bible itself is the most accurate *history book* in the universe. The fact that God wrote the Bible is proof of His interest in passing down history.

Baptists Have Been Ignorant of Their Own Heritage For Many Years.

Read and discuss the following quote.

The following quote is from "The Christian Review," Jan. 1851 by Dr. Sewell S. Cutting:

Lesson One

> No Christian denomination has been so indifferent to its own history as our own.
>
> Our fathers have been left to sleep in unhonored graves. The labors they performed, the sufferings they endured, the heroic characters they bore have alike been forgotten. The books, which amid penury and toil they wrote in defense of their persecuted faith, are almost wholly unknown to those who now possess the noble heritage of religious freedom and Christian truth which they bequeath. It is time for the honor of our name as a Christian people that this indifference were broken up, and that we begin to study for ourselves and to teach our children the lives and deeds of the founders and fathers of our churches.
>
> We hail therefore with delight, any discussion which shall make our brethren acquainted with the early history of their own denomination, or lead them to linger in pious reverence around the graves of those who amid obloquy and contempt first taught the faith we cherish and first established the institutions of religion and learning to which we are so largely indebted.

Dr. Cutting was a Baptist preacher who achieved many great tasks for the Lord. Among his achievements are the following: Baptist pastor in Massachusetts, editor of *The Baptist Advocate*, which became *The New York Recorder*, editor of *The Watchman and*

Reflector, editor of *The Christian Review,* professor of rhetoric and of history at the University of Rochester, secretary of the American Educational Commission, and secretary of the American Baptist Home Mission Society. He was greatly used of God in the promotion of Baptist principles and history. William Cathcart documents in his *Baptist Encyclopedia* that when Cutting took *The Baptist Advocate* and changed it to *The New York Recorder,* "The paper became a great power in promoting the interests of the Baptist denomination."

Lesson One

Review Questions

1. In Joshua chapter 4, the children of Israel were commanded to set up twelve _____ in the Jordan River.

2. God wanted a memorial so that the children of Israel would not _____ what He had done for them.

3. Our _____ seems to have forgotten their own history.

4. We find in Joshua 24 that those who do not remember what God has done in the past could possibly _____ God.

5. Peter has taught us in 2 Peter 1 that it is important to remember because remembering _____ us up.

6. One of the things that stirs us is the testimony of millions of bleeding, dying _____.

7. It is possible that God wants to prepare us for great _____ in our generation.

8. The Book of Acts is a running history of the early _____.

9. Hebrews chapter ____ is another example of God's interest in passing on history.

10. Dr. Sewell S. Cutting said that, "No Christian denomination has been so _____ to its own history as our own."

11. Based on his credentials and ministry experience, do you believe Dr. Cutting was qualified to speak on such issues? _____

12. What year did Dr. Cutting make this statement of our ignorance concerning our Baptist history? _____

Lesson Two
The Problem of Ignorance, How It Happened, and What It Has Produced

---

My people are destroyed for lack of knowledge…
Hosea 4:6a

In our last lesson we examined a statement from Dr. Sewell S. Cutting. The statement pointed out how indifferent Baptists are to their own heritage. The thing to keep in mind as you read this statement is that it was made over 150 years ago. If Dr. Cutting was right about Baptists over 150 years ago, what do you suppose is our condition today? I assure you that in spite of all of the technological and educational advances we've made over the past century and a half, we are in worse condition today than at any other time in history. Baptists are truly ignorant of their own heritage.

Baptist people are in trouble. Everything God warned us about seems to be happening before our eyes. In lesson one, we saw that when we become disconnected from our heritage, we both forget and deny God. We learned that a lack of stirring could be a result of a lack of remembrance. These things are prevalent in our generation.

This lesson will address the problem of ignorance. Before this problem is rectified, it is imperative that several facts be brought to light and accepted. First, Baptists must admit that we are truly ignorant of our history. Secondly, Baptists must understand how this ignorance came about in the first place. Then, we must make sure that we do not allow this to happen again. Lastly, each one of us must do our best to become acquainted with our history, and then commit ourselves to teach it to our children. Every pastor has a great responsibility to train his flock.

Some may ask, "Are we really that ignorant of our heritage?"

We Really Are Ignorant of Our Heritage

The following points prove our lack of knowledge. These are facts that the author has established as true, having done dozens of Baptist Heritage Conferences and having posed these questions to many people. Read and discuss them.

1. Of the over one dozen Baptist people groups that have existed in the church age, most Baptists cannot, off hand, name three of them. Can you?

2. Most professed Baptists cannot give a viable explanation as to why they are Baptists, other than-"Baptists stick closest to the Bible." Can

LESSON TWO

you?

3. The average Baptist today doesn't know when the Baptists began. Do you?

4. Many Baptists believe that the Puritans gave America religious liberty, were a friend to the Baptists, and that without them America would have a state church- none of which are true. Do you know who the Puritans were? Did you know they persecuted our Baptist forefathers? Did you know that they tried to force our Baptist forebears to succumb to a state-church?

5. Many Baptists have not only heard of the Great Awakening, but also wrongly esteem it as the greatest revival in America's history. At the same time, they do not know anything about the Separate Baptist Revival, which was truly the most Scriptural and greatest revival America has ever seen.

6. Most Baptists don't know who started the first Baptist church in America. Do you?

7. Most Baptists don't know that it was Baptists that gave America the Bill of Rights. Did you?

In addition to all this, Baptists have been taught lies as the truth. Namely, that there were no great Baptist evangelists in America's history, and that Baptists are inherently Calvinistic. Both of these are great lies that have been taught as truth and accepted without question by Baptists.

The above is a small representation of the utter ignorance and indifference prevalent among present-day Baptists.

How Did We Become So Separated From Our Baptist Heritage?

History reconstructionists, revisionists, and corrupters. Since Christ began His church, until today, there has been a steady stream of men who have attempted to corrupt and/or destroy the true testimony of the Baptists. William Whitsett, a 19th century Southern Baptist professor, and Rousas H. Rushdoony, a twentieth century author, are just a few of these corrupters.

Our own Baptist schools, for many years, have completely ignored Baptist history in the classroom. This, along with a lack of theological training, has been the downfall of our Baptist schools. A prominent Baptist historian recently stated that, "Baptist history hasn't been properly taught for over 100 years."

The creation of the Fundamentalist Movement has played a major role in destroying our knowledge of Baptist history. For some, this has been a hard saying to accept, but it is absolutely imperative to understand if we are going to restore our testimony to its rightful place.

LESSON TWO

(A) There were 1900 years of Baptist history written before Fundamentalism arose. Baptists were ecclesiastically separated from all non-Baptist groups. Baptists throughout the ages held to certain distinctives that caused them to hold to a rigid separation from error, at any cost.

(B) In the early 1900s the Evangelical Alliance was fighting the battle of German rationalism in their schools. These non-Baptist, Protestant schools were threatened to the point of total apostasy through this heresy.

(C) When the Evangelical Alliance finally took a stand on certain, basic Christian doctrines, many Baptists in their day applauded them.

(D) What happened next was an event that would hurt Baptists in many ways.

(E) The Evangelical Alliance produced the Fundamentalist Movement. Everyone who rejected German rationalism and adhered to certain, basic Bible doctrines was welcomed in the club. Sadly, some Baptists inadvertently turned their backs on ecclesiastical separation and 1900 years of glorious history, and unwisely joined the ranks of Fundamentalism. Remember that these fundamentalist churches were the daughters of Rome, having as their origin and alleged authority, the Protestant Reformation.

(F) The great mistake was for men who already

stood for the whole Bible to join a club that only required you to stand for certain select "fundamentals" of the Bible.

(G) Realize that whenever you emphasize certain truths, you inevitably must de-emphasize others. If some are fundamental, then others are not. If we will separate over some truth, then some truth is not important enough to separate over.

The problem is that doctrinally, the Baptists were already to the right of every Protestant group. Their origins were more pure, and their heritage more rich.

All that could happen in an unscriptural union such as this is that the pure would become unpure. When some Baptists embraced this ecumenical, doctrinally weak fundamentalism, the Baptist faith was hurt in several ways.

What did Fundamentalism do to our Baptist Heritage?

Aside from all of the doctrinal and separation issues, which are very important but not pertinent to this particular study, Fundamentalism effectively severed us from our testimony. Sadly, Baptists turned their backs on 1900 years of Baptist history and inadvertently accepted the relatively short history of Protestantism as their own. This is one of the greatest victories the Devil has ever won. (Please discuss this problem.)

1. Our doctrine has been polluted with a broader, more inclusive, ecumenical twist. An ecumenical spirit, false baptisms (both in mode and authority), a corrupted Lord's table, false church governments, hyper-Calvinism, false Bibles, and other heresies polluted our churches.

2. Our heroes of the faith have been almost exclusively Protestants. We have venerated Moody, Sunday, Torrey, Brainerd, and others while at the same time ignoring John Leland, Obadiah Holmes, Daniel Marshall, Isaac McCoy, and Shubal Stearns. The men that replaced our forefathers, although not wicked men, embraced the typical, doctrinal errors of their Protestant peers.

The need of our generation is to understand what happened to us and to never let it happen again. We have a responsibility to God and our children. We must give our children back their heritage!

Review Questions

1. Over a _____ Baptist groups have existed throughout the church age.

2. The average Baptist doesn't know when the Baptists _____.

3. Who tried to force our Baptist forefathers to succumb to a state church? _____

4. The greatest revival in America's history was the _____ Baptist revival.

5. Baptists gave America the _____ _____ _____.

6. Baptists are not inherently _____.

7. Certain corrupters have rewritten our _____ _____.

8. Baptist history hasn't been taught properly for over _____ years.

9. The _____ Movement has effectively replaced our Baptist heritage with _____ history.

10. There were _____ years of Baptist history before the Fundamentalist Movement ever began.

11. Fundamentalism put forth Protestant _____ in place of our Baptist fore-_____.

12. We have a great responsibility both to _____ and our _____ to perpetuate our great heritage!

Lesson Three
The Baptist Beginning Contrasted with Both Catholic and Protestant Origins

> ...upon this rock I will build my church; and the gates of hell shall not prevail against it.
> **Matthew 16:18b**

The exact origin of the Baptists is a subject prone to producing controversy among believers. Some say that the Baptists began in the seventeen hundreds and were a by-product of the congregational movement or some other splinter group. Others feel generous enough to allow for an English origin in or around the fifteen hundreds. Others feel very sure that the Baptists were produced by the Reformation and are simply kin to the Lutherans, Methodists, Presbyterians, and others. Some Catholics are even generous enough to wrongly admit that the Baptists came out of Romanism at a much earlier date and went headlong into apostasy. With all of these varied opinions to wade through, one might ask- "What is a Baptist to believe?"

The great truth about all of this confusion is that we need not be swayed by any of man's opinions as to the true origin of the Baptists. The infallible

Word of God is all that is needed to ascertain the facts. True scholarly history is also helpful as it never contradicts the Bible, if it is indeed true history.

The author believes that the Baptists are the true, authentic, Biblical Christians. He further believes that it is gross error to say that the Baptists grew out of the Great Reformation period. Baptists don't believe in reform, but rather, in separation from error. Baptists could not have come out of Catholicism, for they were never affiliated with it. Baptists are a separate, ecclesiastical body from all others who claim to be "Christian." The truth is that Catholicism came out of the primitive Baptist churches in the early fourth century. That is to say that when Constantine married the state to the church, the Catholics turned their backs on the truth available in their day.

The Correct Position on Baptist Origins Is Supported by True History

Many reputable historians and scholars believed and taught that the Baptists are the true ancient church.

Look at what others have said about the antiquity of the Baptists:

1. Baptist pastor and Bible scholar, Charles Spurgeon, said:

Lesson Three

> We believe that the Baptists are the original Christians. We did not commence our existence at the Reformation, we were reformers before Luther and Calvin were born; we never came from the Church of Rome, for we were never in it, but we have an unbroken line up to the apostles themselves. We have always existed from the very days of Christ, and our principles, sometimes veiled and forgotten, like a river, which may travel underground for a little season, have always had honest and holy adherents. (April 2, 1861 dedicatory services of new building)

[C.H. Spurgeon, *Metropolitan Tabernacle Pulpit*, VOL. 7, 1861, (Pasadena, Texas, Pilgrim Publications, 1973 reprint), p. 225]

2. Methodist historian, John Clark Ridpath (1840-1900), wrote:

> I should not readily admit that there was a Baptist church as far back as 100 A.D., although without a doubt there were Baptist churches then, as all Christians were then Baptists. (Personal letter to W.A. Jarrel)

[*Baptist Church Perpetuity*, (Dallas, 1894), Reprinted by the Calvary Baptist Church Bookstore, Ashland, Ky., pg. 59]

3. A Catholic, Stanislaus Hosius, Byshop of Wormes in Prussia once wrote:

There shall be no faythe more certayne and true, then is the Anabaptistes, seeyng there be none nowe, or have bene before time fore ye space of these thousand and two hundred years, who have bene more cruelly punyshed, or that have more stoutely, steadfastly, cherefully take theire punishment, yea or have offered them selves of theire owne accorde to deathe, were it never so terrible or grevouse. Yea in Saint Augustyn his time, as he himselffe sayth, there was a certaine monstrouse desire of deathe in them.

[*A Most Excellent treatise of the Begynnyng of Heresyes* (Antwerp: Aeg Diest. 1565, reprint, Yorkshire, England: The Scholar Press Ltd., 1970), p. 44]

Baptist Beginnings (Foundational Ecclesiology)

1. The first mention of the Baptist name in the Word of God is John the Baptist (Matthew 3:1-2).

(A) God named John, "the Baptist," not the Presbyterian or the Methodist or the "Bible churcher." Don't be ashamed of a name that God purposefully named this important figure in His divine plan.

(B) John had a two-fold mission from the Lord.

1. To prepare the way of the Lord (John 1:23).

2. To prepare suitable building materials for the Lord to build His church. He helped prepare the foundation of the church.

Acts 1:22 clearly teaches that God's preparation of the foundation of His church (the Apostles) began with them submitting to the baptism of John the Baptist.

3. John's connection to the Old Testament is obvious in the following verse (Luke 7:26), "A prophet? Yea…"

4. John's ministry in the New Testament is also clearly taught in the Bible.

> a. The "Gospel Age" began with the preaching of John. He did preach the Gospel (John 3:27-36 – "believeth on the son," Acts 19:4 – "that they should believe on Him," Mark 1:1-5 – "Repentance" and "confessing their sins").
>
> b. The following verses further solidify John's New Testament ministry (Matthew 11:13, Luke 16:16).
>
> c. It is crystal clear that God attached the Baptist to the first church.
>
> d. According to Luke 7:29, the apostles had repented and had been baptized by the Baptist. If the publicans were baptized by the Baptist, surely the disciples were. This fact has never been refuted, nor can be (compare to Acts 1:22).

(C) Jesus submitted to baptism by the Baptist (Matthew 3:13-17). Jesus Christ walked approximately 60 miles to be baptized by the only man on earth with the authority to baptize, the **Baptist**. This was N.T. baptism.

(D) The following verses tie both testaments into one ministry (Luke 7:24-29). He was the last O.T. prophet and the first N.T. preacher (especially v. 29 "a prophet…and much more").

2. Jesus took the Baptist apostles and laid them down as the foundation of the church (Ephesians 2:19-20).

(A) The church did not begin on the day of Pentecost. The Holy Ghost is not the founder and head of the church, Jesus Christ is. Jesus is the Cornerstone.

(B) Jesus said He would build His church (Matthew 16:18). This denotes a process that progressed throughout His earthly ministry.

(C) He began to build by calling out and laying down the foundation, a group of baptized believers, prepared by the Baptist.

3. Bible proofs of the first Baptist church before Pentecost.

(A) They fit the definition of a church (a called

out assembly).
(B) Preaching services where Christ both preached and taught (Luke 11:1-13).
(C) They were taught the ordinances of the N.T. church (Luke 22:14-20; Matthew 28:18-20).
(D) They had order. Judas held the bag, as the first treasurer (John 12:1-6).
(E) They were told in Matthew 18:15-17 to tell it to the church.
(F) They worshipped Christ (Matthew 28:17).
(G) They sang hymns (Mark 14:26).
(H) They received the Holy Ghost (John 20:21-23).
(I) They were sent with N.T. authority (John 20:21-23).
(J) They were officially commissioned (Matthew 28:18-20).
(K) The Testator had died (Hebrews 9:15-17).

All of this before the day of Pentecost (and much more). The Holy Ghost's empowerment on the day of Pentecost was the Spirit baptism promised to the church by John in Matthew 3:11. (The church was already there.)

We then read about the church in Jerusalem planting other churches. At the first, all N.T. churches were Scriptural churches, and all practiced the hated ordinance of post-conversion baptism.

The fact that the first church (including Jesus) was built upon men who were baptized by a man that God Himself named the Baptist, and the fact that this name (Baptist) has been impossible to shake down through the ages by those standing for God, and the fact that the church of Jesus Christ, today, is best reflected by Independent, Separated, K.J.B., Baptist churches would definitely cause us to conclude at the very least that the author of history (God) has a purpose in the name Baptist.

Study and discuss the above statement.

It is the name Baptist that has always distinguished us from both Protestants and Catholics.

Review Questions

1. There are several different opinions concerning the _____ of the Baptists.

2. The _____ of God is all that is needed to find the true origin of the Baptists.

3. True _____ _____ is helpful in this study because it never contradicts the Bible.

LESSON THREE

4. The author believes it to be gross error to say that the Baptists came out of the _____ Church or the Great_____.

5. Baptists don't believe in reform, but in _____ from error.

6. Spurgeon believed that the Baptists are the _____ Christians.

7. The other quotes show this same truth, taught by a Methodist and a _____.

8. _____ named John, the Baptist.

9. _____ walked 60 miles for baptism by the Baptist.

10. The _____ were baptized by the Baptist.

11. It is clear that God attached John's ministry to the local N.T. _____.

12. In John 20 it is clear that the church received the Holy Ghost before the day of _____.

13. It is obvious that _____ had a purpose in the name Baptist.

14. It is the name _____ that distinguishes us from both _____ and _____.

Lesson Four
The Waldenses, Successors to the Apostles

> Unto him *be* glory in the church by Christ Jesus throughout all ages, world without end. Amen.
> **Ephesians 3:21**

In this lesson we will begin to trace the baptized believers through the Church Age. As we learn about the various Baptist groups and their faith, we will also learn something about the God of the Bible. Namely, that God has promised to preserve some things for His glory, and He has done just that. We learn early on in Scripture that God promises to preserve Israel. We can clearly see today that He has kept His promise. We also learn in the Bible that God will preserve His Word. We can also see that He has kept His promise in this area as well. What many do not realize is that the same God that promised to preserve Israel and the Bible has also promised to preserve the local church. In the above Scripture, we note that He will have a living testimony at all times in the Church Age. What God preserved was always doctrinally pure and had no affiliation with the false, Catholic institution. The groups we are about to study are this faithful remnant. For those who disagree, the challenge is put forth to produce other groups that more closely follow the New Testament pattern in these particular times in history. There are none. These are the groups who held to Baptist principles, and these are the groups that were slanderously called Rebaptizers (Anabaptists) by the enemies of God. They were called this due to their rejection of the apostate baptism of the establishment, state churches.

In Matthew 16:18 we learn that this faithful remnant not only believed right, but they acted right. They carried out the Great Commission fervently. They are pictured in Matthew 16:18 as a group storming the gates of hell for souls. In Jude 23 these believers, like you and I, were to pull the lost out of the fire! This is a great identifying mark of true churches. They are extremely evangelistic.

If ever there was a group that fit this description, both in sound doctrine and zealous practice, it would have to be our first group of study-the Waldenses. This amazing body of Baptist Christians is truly worthy of serious consideration!

The Waldenses of Italy and France, Successors to the Apostles

One might ask, "What happened to the apostolic churches?" The aim of this lesson is to answer that question.

Lesson Four

1. The period of Polemic. From the martyrdom of Paul to the death of John (A.D. 68-100).

(A) Known by Bible scholars as the "Age of Shadows." Called this because, of all the periods in the history of the church, it is the one about which we know the least.

(B) This was the period of second generation Christians.

Coldness and apostasy was creeping into some of the churches. But not all the churches had gone bad. God had kept His promise and preserved a remnant in Italy and France–the Waldenses.

2. The Waldenses. True Baptist churches dating to A.D. 120 (quite possibly even earlier).

(A) Their antiquity is a proven fact to all who desire truth. The following facts prove the ancient nature of the Waldenses.

1. Hebrews 13:24 – The book of Hebrews was completed by A.D. 95.
A strong testimony of the baptized believers was well established in Italy by then.

2. The existence of the church at Rome, Italy, possibly dates back to the converts of Peter on the day of Pentecost.

3. Paul was also in Rome during his fourth missionary journey – A.D. 59-62, Acts

28:16.

(B) The enemies of the Baptists fight against their antiquity. Some of the strongest voices against the early date for the Waldenses are the Fundamentalists that promote modern versions. They are afraid of accepting an early date for them, as this would also mean an early date for their Bibles.

Many proofs of their antiquity exist. Some are listed below.

1. Rainerio Sacchoni, a former Waldensian preacher who turned away from God and became the Inquisitor of Lombardy, stated: "...Some say that it [the Waldensian schism] dates back to the time of Sylvester (325), others to the time of the apostles."

2. David of Augsburg said, "They call themselves successors of the apostles, and say that they are in possession of the apostolic authority, and of the keys to bind and unbind."

3. The great church historian Neander stated, "The Waldenses of this period asserted the high antiquity of their sect..." He then explains that they believed they existed well before Constantine and the existence of the Roman Catholic Institution.

4. Theodore Beza, the sixteenth century reformer said, "As for the Waldenses, I may be permitted to call them the very seed of the primitive and purer Christian church."

5. Jonathan Edwards, one time president of Princeton University stated, "One of the Popish writers, speaking of the Waldenses, says, the heresy of the Waldenses is the oldest heresy in the world." (We take this as a compliment.)

All the above quotes can be found, along with others, in *A History of the Baptists*, vol. I, chapter 6, p. 3-5 (Texarkana, TX: Bogard Press, 1922), John T. Christian.

(C) They resided in the valleys of the Alps in France and Italy.

(D) The name comes from the Italian word "Valdesi" or the French word "Vaudois," meaning "valley."

(E) They were persecuted fiercely for 1400 yrs.

1. They had more martyrs than any other group of people in history. They were nearly exterminated by Rome.

2. The historian, Boyer, said, "No people of modern times exhibits so much analogy to the ancient Jewish people, as the Vaudois of the Alps of Piedmont; no history has more abounded in marvels than theirs, no church in martyrs."

The following chart is representative of the symbols the Waldenses would carve on cave walls as they fled for their lives from the Roman Catholic Church. Sometimes they lived in these caves for months at a time. When in flight during the dead of winter, the caves offered a warmer temperature than the cold air outside. The alternative was to sleep on the ground. At times the Waldenses would wake up after sleeping on the ground, in the night air, and count dozens of their children who froze to death the previous night.

Lesson Four

Examine the chart and discuss its content.

1. Ancient Signs and Symbols
2. The Light Shining in Darkness
3. The Bush Burning but Not Consumed
4. Struggling and Freeing Oneself
5. The General History of the Evangelistic Churches in the Valley of the Piedmont
6. Papal Crown, Staff Trampled / Anvil Breaking Hammers / Bishop's Crown Trodden
Pope, Exchequer, Inquisitor General

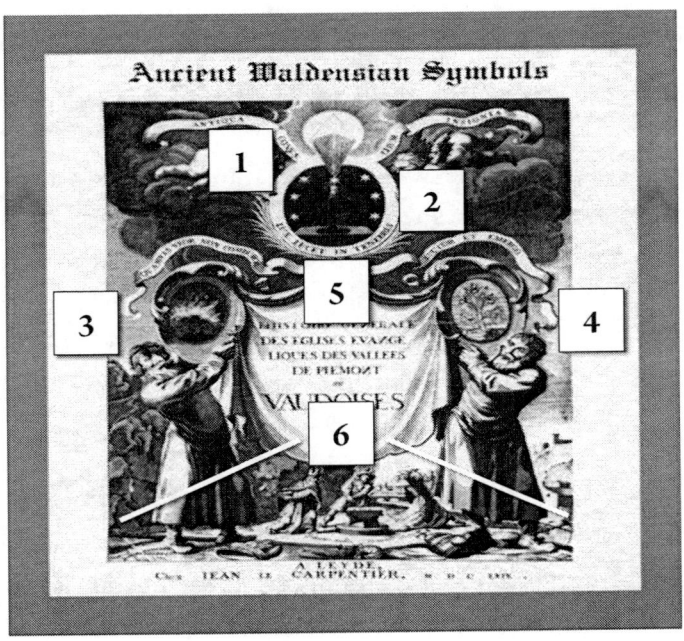

In the previous chart it is clear to see that Waldensian history is saturated in blood. It is a story of hope, faith, and triumph, and yet it is permeated by persecution and sadness. After comparing many assessments from a variety of historians, the author feels as though twenty-five million Waldensian martyrs is a conservative figure.

Hebrews 11:35-39 seems to be a prophetic passage concerning the Waldenses, as it references mountains, caves, and dens. Turn to this passage and see if you can identify the similarities.

(F) Their Doctrine-strikingly Baptist on all major points.
1. Be careful not to let liberals tell you that the ancient Baptist groups were not Baptist at all. Not one group of Baptists on earth totally agrees with another.
We must allow for minor differences among these groups. This is called soul-liberty. Just because they did not follow all of our quirks and traditions is no reason to discredit their standing as ancient Baptists.
2. After having studied their character and devotion to God, coupled with their doctrinal positions, the author believes it is probably a greater stretch to put us in their godly lineage than to put them in ours!

(G) Their Text-
   1. Italic Bible (Itala Biblia) used from A.D. 150. This was used for over a thousand years, kept by the Waldenses, and handed down to become a part of our "Received Text."
   2. The Olivetan Bible was influential in the translation of the Geneva Bible (forerunner of the K.J.B.).

(H) Their Character-They were known to be honest, God fearing, and hard working.

(I) Their memorization of the Scripture.

 William Cathcart in *Baptist Encyclopedia* stated, "The Waldenses loved the Scriptures, could repeat entire books with ease, sometimes the whole New Testament, and were extremely anxious to circulate Bibles..."

(J) Their evangelism.

In the face of great persecution, these churches continued to carry the Gospel. Their traveling salesmen, called peddlers, would go house to house selling tools, carpets, baskets, and other things they had made. If an opportunity arose, they would share the Gospel even though they may have to pay for it with their life.

Would to God we had that kind of love for souls back in our Baptist churches today!

Review Questions

1. God promised to preserve Israel, the Word of God, and the _____ _____.

2. These ancient groups were called Re-_____, or Ana-_____.

3. They were called these names because they rejected the _____ _____ of the state churches.

4. The Waldenses of Italy and France are the successors to the _____.

5. The antiquity of the Waldenses is a _____ fact.

6. Some Fundamentalists fight against the antiquity of the Waldenses because it exposes the _____ versions.

7. *A History of the Baptists,* by John T. _____, documents the early date for the Waldenses.

8. The Waldenses resided in the _____ of the _____ in France and Italy.

Lesson Four

9. Sometimes the Waldenses lived in caves for _____ at a time.

10. Twenty-five _____ Waldensian martyrs is a conservative figure.

11. The Waldensian text of Scriptures is represented in history through the _____ Bible and the _____ Bible.

12. William Cathcart stated that sometimes the Waldenses could repeat the entire New _____.

13. The evangelistic salesmen were called Waldensian _____.

Lesson Five
The Novatians and Montanists

> Lord, thou hast been our dwelling place in all generations.
> **Psalm 90:1**

The previous lesson detailed the ancient Baptist group called the Waldenses. In this lesson we will examine two more ancient Baptist groups, the Montanists and the Novatians. These two groups held to Baptist principles and were representative of Christ's true churches in the early centuries of Baptist Christianity. This is not to say that they were the only true churches, for we know that there were Waldensian assemblies during this timeframe also. It is important to interject an important fact here: namely, that as we go through our study, we must be careful not to view these groups as the only true churches in their respective timeframes. The Waldenses would remain true to Baptist principles for around fifteen centuries. The Albigenses and Paulicians would also exist as true churches for centuries. In addition to this, there may have been many assemblies that were quite unknown except to those in their immediate areas. History is "sketchy" at places and therefore we are just not sure where all of God's true congregations were.

An honest assessment of history tells us two things that are for certain. The first is that there have always been churches that held to the Word of God as their only rule of faith and practice. The second fact is that there has always been a manifold testimony of Christ's true churches. That is to say, that there were various churches in various places in every age. These churches resided in various places at the same time. There has never been a time when this was not the case.

Now, we continue our study of the ancient Baptists by examining these two faithful groups of baptized believers-the Montanists and the Novatians.

The Novatians & Montanists

Grouped together because they arose around the same timeframe. The Montanists date back to A.D. 175 and the Novatians date back to A.D. 250.

1. The Montanists (A.D. 175).

(A) They began in Phrygia (now modern day Turkey) and spread to Europe and Africa.

(B) A man named Montanus, a priest of the pagan cult of Cybele, was saved in A.D. 150. There is a reoccurring event that takes place throughout the church age, namely, that God has seen fit to take the vilest of sinners and save them. He then puts them into the ministry. Often these wicked sinners make the best preachers and are brightly shining trophies of God's grace. This was the case with the Apostle Paul, and this would also be the case with Montanus.

(C) He saw the churches slipping and in A.D. 157 began to preach against three things:
1. Ritualism.
The problem of ritualism began thousands of years ago. It was a standard part of what the Lord calls "the doctrine of Jezebel." However, Jezebel was not the only one guilty of ritualism. This error would resurface time and again throughout church history and attempt to be as good as or better than salvation. This heresy would attempt to prop up religion. Ritualism tries to authenticate dead religion by busying the individual and impressing the observer with churchy activity. Eventually, Rome would embrace ritualism as part of their system of works. The Devil has used rituals to try to authenticate Catholicism as a replacement of the true faith. Montanus stood against dead religion and all of its rituals and fanfare. Every Baptist preacher must

guard against ritualism in the churches, like Montanus did.

2. Nicolaity.

a. Nicolaity is the heresy that states that there are different classes of Christians: the upper class and the lower class. The upper class under this system has sole authority to interpret Scripture, make up rules, impose duties, and bind heavy burdens that are "grevious to be bourne" upon the lower class.

b. Look up Revelation 2:15 to see how Jesus feels about this type of activity.

3. Laxness in discipline and church membership standards.

a. Church discipline is commanded in the Word of God. Membership standards are taught in the same texts.

b. Look up and discuss these references: Matthew 18:15-17, 1 Corinthians 5:1-13.

(D) Followers arose, called Montanists.

Often people stumble at the names of the various groups of Baptist Christians. For example, if one did not know better, he may wrongly believe that Montanus must have been a proud fellow to have named this group the Montanists. The truth is that Montanus did not name this group, just as Arnold of Brescia did not name the Arnoldists, nor did Peter DeBruys name the Petrobrussians. The names we use to identify these groups are often the names that were used by their enemies. These names would be used so frequently that they, by default, became the historical tags for these groups of baptized believers.

(E) The Montanists influenced the rise of the Novatians.

(F) No other group of Baptists has been attacked by modern day religionists and believers so regularly as the Montanists. This attack is based upon their supposed doctrinal extremes. They, like every other group of Baptists in history, held to certain positions that other Baptist groups would see a little differently. But on all the major points of doctrine, they were historic Baptists, holding to those principles that identify Baptist churches through the ages.

> **1. Please be careful when studying Baptist history that you are reading after historians with the right theology.** The vast majority of these unwarranted attacks come from religious liberals who oppose the perpetuity of churches and effectively deny Christ's

promises of the same.

2. John Taylor Christian's *History of the Baptists* is a trusted source of information on the Montanists.

3. When you do find places of disagreement with a particular group of believers, please allow the same soul liberty that you would expect others to have with you concerning minor issues of faith or practice. Soul liberty is an important Baptist distinctive, and all too often it is not practiced in our ranks. Soul liberty is that doctrine that states that all men must have full religious freedom to worship God according to the dictates of their own conscience. This also allows for unbelief. Baptists suffered at the hands of Rome for over a thousand years and were never granted soul liberty by the oppressors. We must not practice manipulation of any kind that would seek to control the belief and/or practice of our Baptist brethren. If we do, we are no better than Rome.

(G) Tertullian was a devoted scholar in the school at Alexandria. He was converted, and for many years was a leader of a congregation of Montanists. He lived from A.D. 160 to 230 and defended Christianity for many years.

Moller, contributor to the *Shaff-Herzog Religious Encyclopedia*, wrote,

> But Montanism was, nevertheless, not a new form of Christianity; nor were the Montanists a new sect. On the contrary, Montanism was, simply a reaction of the old, the primitive church, against the obvious tendency of the day, to strike a bargain with the world and arrange herself comfortably in it.

2. The Novatians (A.D. 250).

(A) The Novatians, like many Baptist groups, arose as a result of people who wanted to stay true to Bible doctrine.

(B) Novatian was born around A.D. 180. He was saved around A.D. 250.

(C) Novatian, the pastor at Rome, became enraged when apostates once rejected from the church were allowed back into the fold.

(D) Novatian and his followers espoused Baptist doctrine. They emphasized the following points:

    1. Purity of church membership.
    2. Rigid church discipline.
    3. Rebaptism of apostates.
    4. Scriptural baptism.
        a. By immersion.
        b. For mature adults.
        c. Without great ceremony.

d. On church authority.

William Cathcart stated the following on page 862, Vol. 2, in his *Baptist Encyclopedia*,

> Novatian himself was a man of fervent piety; and his life after his conversion was above reproach, unless when accusations came from a calumniator whose charges were incapable of proof. He was the author of works on "The Passover," "Circumcision," "The Sabbath," "High-Priests," "The Trinity," and on other subjects. He had many distinguished men among his disciples. His community spread very widely, and enjoyed special prosperity in Phrygia; but declined rapidly in the fifth century. The Novatians, as a people, were an honor to Christianity, and their teachings and example exercised a powerful restraint upon the growing corruptions of the old church. The Novatians commenced their denominational life when the baptism of an unconscious babe was unknown outside of Africa; and there it had a limited, if not a doubtful, existence. Indeed, if a celebrated letter of Cyprian, about a council of bishops, said to have been held in Carthage half a dozen years after Novatian set up his banner of church purity, be a forgery, and the supposition is by no means an improbable one, unconscious infant baptism has no proof of its existence in the literature of the world. The infant rite, according to the letter of Cyprian just referred to, had Cyprian for its patron, and as he had shown the utmost hostility to Novatian, he and his followers would not be very eager to adopt a ceremony of

Lesson Five

which his letter, if genuine, shows that he was the special friend. These considerations, together with the holiness of life demanded by Novatian churches, have led many persons to regard them as Baptists. Of the truth of this opinion in the early history of this people there can be no doubt; and that the majority of their churches baptized only instructed persons to the end of their history is in the highest degree probable.

(E) The doctrinal stand of the Novatians caused a division among the ranks of Christendom in A.D. 251.

(F) The Novatians rejected the apostate baptism of the establishment churches.

(G) The Novatians had a great influence on France.

(H) Historians agree that, interspersed with some Montanists, this group of baptized believers survived to at least the sixth century.

There were several similarities between the Montanists and the Novatians. This is partly because they were trying to follow the same Book, and partly because they were both battling the apostasy that was prevalent in their day. Both groups were

strong in these areas:
- Strong on church membership and commitment
- Strong on post conversion immersion
- Strong on soul liberty
- Strong against ecclesiastical hierarchies

Baptists today should firmly defend these same truths!

Review Questions

1. The _____ and _____ arose around the same timeframe.

2. There has always been a _____ testimony of Christ's true churches in every time frame of history.

3. _____ was an occult priest before his conversion.

4. What three things did Montanus preach against fervently? _____, _____, and _____.

5. Ritualism has its roots in the doctrine of _____.

6. Nicolaity takes away the right of the people to _____ Scripture for themselves.

7. Church _____ is commanded in the Word of God.

8. Soul liberty means that all men have freedom to worship God according to the dictates of their own _____. It also allows men freedom to remain in _____.

9. _____ was once a devoted scholar in the school of Alexandria.

10. _____ was a pastor in Rome.

11. The Novatians emphasized:

_____
_____
_____
_____
_____

12. What four things constituted scriptural baptism to the Novatians?

_____
_____
_____
_____

13. Did William Cathcart believe the Novatians were Baptists? Yes / No

14. What country did the Novatians influence greatly? _____.

15. The Novatians survived to at least the _____ century.

16. Write out the four similarities between the Montanists and the Novatians.

_____
_____
_____
_____

Lesson Six
The Donatists and Paulicians

> I will remember the works of the LORD: surely I will remember thy wonders of old.
>
> **Psalm 77:11**

In our previous lessons we discussed many doctrinal issues as well as three major Baptist groups. We also briefly mentioned the persecutors of the Baptists, the Roman Catholic Institution. In this lesson, we will address more doctrinal issues, discuss two more Baptist groups, and examine in depth, this great enemy of liberty of conscience, Roman Catholicism. It was during the timeframe we are presently examining, that this blood-thirsty, religious cult experienced its illegitimate birth. This is not to say that there was no persecution before A.D. 315. There was persecution. We know that the first Baptist, John, was beheaded. We also know that the apostles were martyred for preaching Christ. Our Lord was beaten and crucified. This was the beginning of Baptist Christianity, and it was bloody and sorrowful from its very beginning.

The timeframe that would immediately follow the apostles' ministry would continue to be a dark time of persecution. Before Roman Catholicism ever got off the ground, imperial Roman persecutions were carried out. Diocletian was one of the most fierce persecutors of the baptized believers. He had a column erected in his kingdom with these words inscribed: "Extincto nominee Christorium." This meant that, "The name of Christianity will become extinct." He then tried as best as he could to do so but failed. Later came the false universal church. Roman Catholicism, by far, would become the most ungodly, bloodthirsty organization on earth.

In our present study, we are standing at the doorway to the Dark Ages. What lies behind this historical doorway was the Devil's best attempt to destroy the church of the Lord Jesus Christ. He, like Diocletian, failed too. As you begin to study the Dark Ages and learn of the sad atrocities that were commonplace during this era, take heart in several facts. First, remember that these innocent martyrs were and are known of our Lord. The Word of God states in Psalm 116:15, "Precious in the sight of the LORD is the death of his saints." They entered His eternal presence upon their deaths. Secondly, realize that nearly every time that Baptist, Christian blood was spilled, those drops of blood became the seeds of new churches in new areas. Others were strengthened and emboldened as they watched their brethren make the ultimate sacrifice for a worthy Saviour.

Lesson Six

Consequently, they went and preached Christ, and new works were started. This leads us to our third encouraging fact: namely, that God will stir you up by way of remembrance through your examination of the Dark Ages. How any believer could study the great sacrifice made by the Baptists, and not be stirred, remains a mystery! So as you examine these facts, let them change your heart. As you see their love for God, examine yours. As you read of their willingness to evangelize in the face of certain death, let it give you a renewed zeal to witness for our Lord! Finally, remember that we will meet them all someday, every last one of them. What a day that will be!

1. The Donatists (A.D. 311).

(A) Donatus lived from approximately 280 to 355.

(B) In A.D. 311 Donatus protested at an ordination in Carthage, North Africa. The ordainer and candidate were both proven to have surrendered Bibles to be burned in Imperial persecutions. The men, that had surrendered Bibles while under pressure, found no sympathy with Donatus. Donatus knew that there were women and children who were willing to be sliced in pieces for Christ. Because of this, Donatus found these grown men unworthy of the office of a bishop after having turned their backs on Christ when put to the test.

(C) Doctrinally, and in other ways, the Donatists were much like the Novatians.

(D) They believed that they were the only true kind of church in northern Africa.

(E) They denied the right of the state to persecute on behalf of the establishment church.

(F) They rebaptized all who came to them from the Roman Catholic Institution.

Important Fact:
The Roman Catholic Institution was established during this timeframe. Under the leadership of the Emperor Constantine, the Edict of Milan passed in A.D. 313. At this time, state (Rome) and religion became entangled in an unholy union. The Roman emperor, Constantine, supposedly granted freedom to Christians. Not long after this event, the persecution of the Baptists picked up. This new state-church monster would become drunken with the blood of the martyrs (Revelation 17).

Turn to Revelation 17 and examine the follow-

Lesson Six

ing indicators. These clues prove beyond a shadow of a doubt that the great whore of Revelation is the Roman Catholic Institution. Notice the similarities:

1. Sitteth upon many waters
2. The kings of the earth committed fornication with her
3. The inhabitants of the earth made drunk with the wine of her fornication
4. Scarlet colored beast
5. Seven heads
6. Arrayed in purple and scarlet color
7. Decked with gold, precious stones, and pearls
8. Having a golden cup in her hand
9. Drunken with the blood of the saints and martyrs of Jesus
10. The seven heads are seven mountains on which the woman sitteth.

It is interesting to note that if someone cannot identify Rome from this long list of clues, the Lord makes sure they know it is Rome with His last clue. Historically speaking, there is only one city that has been referred to as the "City on Seven Hills." That city is Rome.

Discuss #9 (from the list of identifying marks of Catholicism) in class. What does it mean to be drunk? What people in history had the most martyrs? _____ What organization martyred more people than any other organization in history? _____

2. The Paulicians (A.D. 660).
(A) Called Paulicians for two reasons:
>1. They placed a strong emphasis on the Epistles of Paul.
>2. They adopted Pauline names for their leaders.

(B) Many historians claim apostolic origin of these churches.

Gibbon stated in his classic book, *The Rise and Fall of the Roman Empire*, "The faith of the Paulicians stemmed to the first century and was a branch of Antiochan Christianity."

It was common in England, centuries later, for the Anabaptists to be slanderously called Paulicians.

(C) The Paulicians rose to prominence around A.D. 660 with the conversion and subsequent leadership of a man named Constantine.
>1. This man lived from 630-687 and is not connected to Constantine of Roman Catholic fame, of which we have just spoken.

Lesson Six

2. Constantine was from Armenia, a mountainous region which is now modern-day Turkey.

The persecutions against the Paulicians were fierce. Benjamin Evans stated:

> What the pen failed to do, the sword of the magistrate effected. The Novatians, the Donatists, and others that followed them, are examples. Many of them taught those peculiar views of Christian ordinances which are special to us as Baptists. Beyond all doubt such views were inculcated by the Paulicians, the primitive Waldenses, and their brethren. Over Europe they were scattered, and their converts were numerous, long before the Reformation shed its light on the darkness of Europe.
>
> (*The Early English Baptists,* Benjamin Evans, 1862, Vol. 1, pgs. 1, 2, 1977 reprint).

(D) To become a Paulician pastor was the equivalent of wearing a target on your chest.
When they entered the ministry they were asked,

> "...Art thou then able to drink the cup which I am about to drink, or to be baptized with the baptism with which I am about to be baptized?"

To which they would reply, "...I take on myself scourgings, imprisonments, tortures, reproaches, crosses, blows, tribulation and all temptations of the world..." (Broadbent, Op. Cit., pp. 53, 54.)

(E) All Eastern emperors persecuted the Paulicians. The worst persecutions were those initiated by the Empress Theodora and her son Michael III (A.D. 842-867). During these 25 years over 100,000 Paulicians were slain. They were drowned, beheaded, burnt, and killed in many other merciless ways.

Depiction of the bloody Empress Theodora

Lesson Six

(F) Although Rome thought up many false charges against them, history proves that their doctrine was Baptist Bible doctrine.

(G) Persecutions sent them fleeing into several eastern European countries.

(H) Their prominence lasted well over 400 yrs.

Review Questions

1. The beginning of Baptist Christianity was both _____ and _____.

2. Diocletian had a column in his kingdom with these words inscribed on it, "_____ _____ _____."

3. The above words meant, "The name of _____ will become _____."

4. Diocletian carried out _____ persecutions.

5. In your own words, write out two reasons we can be encouraged even though there were so many

innocent martyrs killed.

_____
_____
_____
_____
_____

6. Donatus protested at an _____ in Carthage, North Africa.

7. The Donatists were much like the _____.

8. The Donatists _____ all who came to them from the Roman Catholic Institution.

9. The emperor, _____, married state and church together.

10. The Edict of _____ passed in A.D. 313.

11. Revelation ____ gives us a clear description of _____ Catholicism.

12. Rome is the "_____ that sits on _____ _____."

LESSON SIX   69

13. Throughout the Dark Ages, the Roman Catholic Institution was drunken with the _____ of the _____ and with the _____ of Jesus.

14. Give two reasons as to why the seventh century Baptists were called Paulicians.

_____
_____
_____
_____
_____

15. Gibbon stated that the faith of the Paulicians stemmed to the _____ century. He also said it was a "_____ of _____ Christianity."

16. Becoming a Paulician pastor was the equivalent of wearing a _____ on your _____.

17. The Empress _____ and her son _____ killed over _____ Paulicians in a 25 year period.

Lesson Seven
The Albigenses

> Our fathers trusted in thee: they trusted, and thou didst deliver them. They cried unto thee, and were delivered: they trusted in thee, and were not confounded.
>
> **Psalms 22:4-5**

In lesson seven, we will turn our focus to one major Baptist group, the Albigenses. Aside from the Waldenses, this may be the most important group of baptized believers in history. To the Waldenses goes the sad legacy of having more martyrs in sheer numbers than any other group in history, whether it be a secular or religious group. To the Albigenses, one must look to discover that they had more martyrs by percentage than all other people groups in history. They were slaughtered in wholesale fashion by the anti-Christ, Roman Catholic Institution. In this lesson, we will examine their life, legacy, and love for God.

Also, notice the map of greatest persecution that is included in this lesson. Look this over and acquaint yourself with key towns and cities. You will want to remember where Albi is, as well as Rome, and other cities. These cities are all listed on the map legend.

This lesson will also deal with a timeframe known as the Dark Ages. There is much confusion today surrounding this era, and we will attempt to set the record straight on this important subject. One cannot fully understand history itself without truly grasping an honest understanding of the Dark Ages. So, open your mind to the facts and your heart to the Lord. If you do, this lesson will surely "stir you up!"

The Albigenses (A.D. 700)

(A) Named for the southern French town of Albi. This area was known for dissent and resistance to the "Holy Mother Church" (see map).

(B) Some historians trace the Albigenses back to the Paulicians. Others say they existed since N.T. times in southern France. The author's personal opinion is that they may have been migrated Waldenses. Under persecution, the Waldenses would often flee for their lives and find refuge in the countryside far away.

The historian Faber wrote this concerning the Albigenses and their place in Baptist history:

Lesson Seven

From the apostolic age itself down to the present that venerable Church has been seated in the Valleys of the Cottian Alps. There it has never ceased to profess one and the same unvarying Theological System. Thus faithfully reflecting the sincere unadulterated Gospel of primitive Christianity: and there, both ecclesiastically and morally, the practice of its members has happily corresponded with their religious profession. This very remarkable Church forms in the first instance, the chain of connection, between the Primitive Church and the Church of the Albigenses...

(*The History of the Ancient Vallenses and Albigenses*, George Stanley Faber, 1838 (from 1990 reprint), preface pgs. II, III, & XI.)

(C) God blessed them, and they spread rapidly through southern France.

1. Their influence concerned the Catholic Institution.

2. First, the Catholics attempted to convert them through ecclesiastical conversion. This would not work because the Albigenses knew the Word of God.

3. They were then falsely accused by Rome to be Manichaeans (as were the Paulicians and the Waldenses). Rome used this as a reason to persecute them. This alleged heresy was a cross between Persian-Zoroastrianism and

Gnosticism.

4. Next, Rome would turn to merciless persecutions.

> a. In A.D. 1139, Lateran II condemned them as heretics. The Council of Tours did the same in 1163.
>
> b. Organized crusades against the Albigenses have been termed as "one of the black spots of history."
>
> c. In one instance, the town of Beziers was before the attacking armies. Rather than seek out the Albigenses from among the Catholic populace, the papal authority gave the order to "kill them all. The Lord knows His own." The heartless soldiers obeyed. All were slain, including women and children. Almost 20,000 were murdered in bloody fashion in this one attack.
>
> d. The slaughters continued and grew worse (if that is imaginable) as the Dominicans were put in charge of the Inquisition. The Dominicans were known as the "Pope's Hounds."
>
> **Catholic Societies.** Throughout the years the Romanists thought it necessary to raise up secretive, loyal, blood-thirsty societies. The Dominicans was one such

Lesson Seven

society. Dominican means "God's Dogs." When believers such as the Albigenses, and earlier their Waldensian counterparts, would run up into the mountains for their lives and escape, this would frustrate the papal hierarchy. The Dominicans were suppose to sniff out our Baptist forefathers and kill every last one, like dogs tearing apart a helpless rabbit. They were merciless killers. They did it all in the name of God. The Jesuits and Franciscans were some of the other prominent anti-heresy societies. The Jesuits were known to have been good at infiltrating Baptist assemblies, often by making a false profession. Then, when they knew where the believers lived, this information was taken to the papal authorities and the Catholic armies of slaughter would carry out the persecution.

e. Pope Innocent III launched a total of four crusades to exterminate the Albigenses. In 1209, about 60,000 unarmed civilians were slain. All were killed, including the elderly, women, children, and even babies. Christians were cast from high places. They were chased into caves and smothered with fires set at the entrance.

They were torn to pieces by dogs, torn to pieces with large pliers called prongs, torn apart on racks, disemboweled, and had hot metal poured down their throats. They were burned at the stake, crucified upside down, and drowned.

f. In 1234, Pope Gregory IV raised a German army to kill several hundred thousand more Albigenses near Breman & Oldenburg- all in the name of God.

(D) The Albigenses have one of the saddest stories in the history of N.T. churches. The greater part of them shed their blood for the cause of Christ.

1. So widespread and devastating were these crusades, that the testimony of Christ was all but exterminated in southern France.

2. Those who did escape with their lives fled to Italy and Germany where they further sowed seeds for the Anabaptist movement in Europe.

3. The Albigenses were probably the basis of Bogomilism.

Dark Ages. As has been mentioned, a proper understanding of the Dark Ages is needed for the student of Baptist history to fully understand the

Lesson Seven

whole of history itself. First, one must be willing to let go of preconceived ideas concerning this subject. It is also important to note that the world has twisted the truth about the Dark Ages in their books and in their classroom teachings. The opinions of the lost must not bear upon one's understanding of the Dark Ages.

The Dark Ages was not simply a time when no great inventions came forth. Nor was it just a period in which no great music was composed and no great art painted. This is the candy-coated rendition of history that the world wants you to swallow.

The Dark Ages was the horrible timeframe in history that spanned over a thousand years (including the Middle Ages, this timeframe began around 400 and lasted into the sixteenth century). During these dark centuries the Bible was the forbidden Book. All dissent was punishable by torture, banishment, dismemberment, burning, and a host of other cruelties. The whole European continent was dominated by the Roman Catholic Empire. Their theology dictated their actions. This theological system is known as Augustinianism. Augustine was a Roman Catholic theologian. He believed that the Catholic Institution was the spiritual city of God on earth, and to secure its earthly kingdom, all enemies must be eliminated. This is also known as Dominion theology as it promotes dominating others as opposed to evangelizing others. Their goal is to rule the world for God. During the Dark Ages, the entire European continent was imprisoned by this wicked institution and its theological system. The Baptists suffered loss so great during this era that we cannot fully understand its magnitude on this side of Heaven!

"...they wandered in deserts, and in mountains, and in dens and caves of the earth." (Heb. 11:38)

Lesson Seven

Augustine was born in A.D. 354.

He was influenced by platonic doctrines and developed much of the Roman Catholic doctrinal system.

Review Questions

1. The _____ had a larger percentage of martyrs than any other group of people in history.

2. The Albigenses were named for the southern French town of _____.

3. The Albigenses may have been migrated _____.

4. The Catholics attempted to convert the Albigenses through _____ conversion.

5. The Albigenses were falsely accused of being _____.

6. Organized crusades against the Albigenses have been termed as _____ _____.

7. The _____ were known as the "Pope's Hounds."

8. The _____ and _____ were other prominent Catholic societies.

Lesson Seven

9. Pope Innocent III launched four crusades in an attempt to _____ the Albigenses.

10. In 1209 about _____ unarmed civilians were slain.

11. Pope Gregory IV raised a German army to kill _____ _____ _____ more Albigenses.

12. The testimony of Christ was all but _____ in southern France.

13. The Albigenses were probably the basis of _____.

14. Without an understanding of the _____ _____, it is impossible to understand the whole of history itself.

15. In your own words, write a short paragraph describing what the Dark Ages was not.

_____
_____
_____
_____

_____
_____
_____
_____

16. A man named _____ developed the Roman Catholic system.

17. Augustinianism is also known as _____ theology.

18. In your own words, write a short paragraph describing what the Dark Ages was.

_____
_____
_____
_____
_____
_____
_____
_____
_____

Lesson Eight
The Bogomils, Paterines, and Henricians

> Thus saith the LORD, Stand ye in the ways, and see, and ask for the old paths, where *is* the good way...
> **Jeremiah 6:16a**

Lesson eight is a concise overview of three Baptist groups. These groups are the Bogomils, Paterines, and the Henricians. The timeframe covered in this particular study lies between the eighth and thirteenth centuries. This was a time of great darkness across the European continent. It was so dark and spiritually devoid that is has been named "The Midnight of the Dark Ages." In this section of history we discover unimaginable blasphemies and wickedness embraced and performed by Rome. This dark span of centuries, because of the abominations carried out by the Roman Catholic Institution, has been referred to by more than one historian as the "Pornocracy." Dueling popes, sodomy, rape, incest, prostitution, and religious acts that seem to have been invented to anger God were the fare of this day.

In the midst of all of this darkness, a light shined. In fact, there were many little lights trying desperately to simply follow their Saviour. The Bogomils,

Paterines, and Henricians were these lights. In the grand scheme of the church age, this was the era in which men lost heart as to their hope for religious liberty. These Baptists did not lose desire for liberty of conscience, but many could not understand how it could ever come to pass.

Imagine standing in a tunnel that is pitch black. Now imagine that this tunnel is a thousand miles long, and you are standing in the center. In such a situation we can only begin to understand what our forebears experienced. They had seen nothing but bloodshed, burnings, and torture for hundreds of years. Generation after generation longed to be free to worship such as you and I do today. When they looked around or into the future it must have been difficult to see how God's people would ever be free to worship Him. Their only comfort was God's Spirit and God's Word. To these they clung, and for these they died. We must never forget this noble company, for it was they who blazed the trail we stand on today. They carved it out with faith, hope, and charity. And they never ceased to proclaim the greatest story ever told.

1. The Bogomils (A.D. 720).

(A) The rise of this group took place around A.D. 720. They survived for several centuries.

Lesson Eight

Broadbent, in the conclusion of his church history, wrote:

> There have in all times been brethren who...have been called by many names, Cathars, Novatians, Paulicians, Bogomils, Albigenses, Waldenses, Lollards, Anabaptists ... and others innumerable, many congregations also of Baptists ...; they have been one in their endeavour to act upon the New Testament and to follow the example of the New Testament churches.

(*The Pilgrim Church*, E.H. Broadbent, 1931, pg. 89.)

(B) They inhabited Bulgaria and would later flee, under persecution, to the Balkan countries.
(C) Two groups influenced the rise of the Bogomils.
    1. The Albigenses, as have already been mentioned.
    2. The Paulicians. When the Paulicians went to Bulgaria, they became known as Bogomils, thus evaporating into that group.
(D) The name, Bogomils, is thought to have meant, "Friends of God."
(E) They were persecuted, as all other Baptist groups.
    1. Pope Innocent III tried to eradicate them.

2. He launched a Dominican and Franciscan Inquisition against them.
   3. They endured many enemies, even though many died at the hands of the blood thirsty Dominicans and Franciscans.

(F) They were in favor of a very simple brand of Christianity.

(G) They spread the Gospel as much as possible, in spite of the opposition.

2. The Paterines (They began between 1000 & 1040).

(A) By the year 1040 they were numerous and conspicuous at Milan. Their presence in this area is well documented at over 200 yrs. in duration.

(B) The Paterines are in the lineage of the other major Baptist groups.
William Wall stated:

> Beside the name of Berengarians, other names that were severally used at several places and times, were these: Cathari (or Puritans), Paterines, Petrobrussians, Lyonists, Albigenses, Waldenses, and several more.
>
> (*The History of Infant Baptism*, William Wall, MDCCCXXXVI, Vol. 2, pgs. 238, 239.)

(C) They are known to have been people who

emphasized personal separation.
  1. They were decent in their deportment.
  2. They were modest in their dress and discourse.
  3. Their morals were irreproachable.
(D) It was said that the state did not trouble them. The clergy, however, preached, prayed, and published books against them with unabated zeal.
(E) They stood firmly against the Roman Catholic Institution in a region saturated by Catholic influence.
  1. They called the crucifix (the cross with Christ still hanging on it), "The abomination of desolation standing in the holy place."
  2. They said the crucifix was "the mark of the beast."
  3. They were most well known for their stand for scriptural baptism.
(F) Their doctrine was Baptist doctrine.

3. The Henricians (A.D. 1116).

(A) They were called Henricians by their enemies.
(B) Henry of Lousanne, Switzerland, was a former Benedictine monk.
  1. He became well known for his fiery, street preaching against the sins of the clergy.

2. In 1116 he entered the city of Mans on the first day of Lent. He preached publicly against the worship of saints, infant baptism, works salvation, and the corruption of the clergy. Revival broke out here, as it did in many other cities.

(C) In Mans the inferior clergy became his followers, and the people followed him and his doctrine. Many embraced the truth even though it meant endangering their lives.

Phillip Schaff notes that one of the results of Henry's preaching was that, "Women of loose morals repented and young men were persuaded to marry them."

(D) Henry was allowed to die of starvation in prison, possibly in Rheims.

Lesson Eight

The above picture depicts an ancient underground prison. Many of our forebears starved to death in cold, damp, dark chambers similar to this one.

Review Questions

1. Lesson eight covers what three groups? _____, _____, and _____.

2. The timeframe covering the eighth through the thirteenth centuries is known as the "_____ of the _____ Ages."

3. Because of the utter wickedness of Romanism during this timeframe, some historians refer to this era as the "_____."

4. Obtaining religious _____ must have seemed unfathomable during the "Midnight of the Dark Ages."

5. The only comfort God's people had during this time came through His _____ and His _____.

6. The _____ inhabited Bulgaria.

7. Under persecution, the Bogomils fled to the _____ countries.

Lesson Eight

8. Tradition teaches that the name Bogomils meant "_____ of _____."

9. Pope _____ tried to eradicate the Bogomils.

10. The Paterines emphasized _____ _____.

11. The Paterines called the crucifix, "_____ _____ _____."

12. The Paterines said that the _____ was the "Mark of the Beast."

13. Henry of _____, _____, was a former _____ _____.

14. What were the results of Henry's public preaching? _____ _____.

15. When revival broke out, women of loose morals _____ and young men were persuaded to _____ _____.

16. How did Henry die?

_____

LESSON NINE
The Petrobrussians and Arnoldists

> One generation shall praise thy works to another, and shall declare thy mighty acts.
> **Psalm 145:4**

Lesson nine briefly brings to light two, twelfth century, Baptist people groups. These congregations were home to some of the boldest Baptist ministers that ever lived. Peter de Bruys and Arnold of Brescia were both great preachers and great overall leaders of the Baptists. In these two men we clearly see several things. First, we see God's desire to change people by His grace and then use them in the ministry. Secondly, we see the true character and bravery of these men. They did not just talk the talk, they walked the walk. Both men died for what they believed. Many of their followers did also. This was a noble bunch. Thirdly, we see the Roman Church at its lowest point in human history. It had become such a laughingstock among the common populace that discontent was the feeling of the day. So many were disgruntled with the hypocrisy of Rome that when these two men and their preacher friends began to publicly herald the pure Gospel, everything from riots to revivals broke out regularly. These two men, and the many baptized believers of their day, truly gave the Devil a black eye and snatched thousands of souls from his clutches. Rome patiently bided her time until the wretched cult could grab these great men of God and martyr them in a most cruel fashion. History has not forgotten these two men and their influence. Would to God that, like our Bible verse states, we would not let their memory die, but would do everything in our power to share their testimony with the next generation.

1. The Petrobrussians (A.D. 1126).
(A) Named after Peter de Bruys, a converted Catholic priest and solid Gospel preacher.
(B) His ministry was primarily in southern France.
(C) His doctrine was definitely of the Baptist line. He and his followers abhorred the errors of the Roman, universal, Catholic Institution!
William Cathcart reported the following in his *Baptist Encyclopedia:*

> He [Peter de Bruys] taught that baptism was of no advantage to infants, and that only believers should receive it, and he gave a new baptism to all his converts; he condemned the use of churches and altars, no doubt for the idolatry practiced in them; he denied that the body and blood of Christ are to be

Lesson Nine

found in the bread and wine of the Supper, and he taught that the elements on the Lord's table are but signs of Christ's flesh and blood; he asserted that the offerings, prayers, and good works of the living could not profit the dead, that their state was fixed for eternity the moment they left the earth; like the English Baptists of the seventeenth century, and like the Quakers of our day, he believed that it was wrong to sing the praises of God in worship; and he rejected the adoration of crosses, and destroyed them wherever he found them.

It is said that on a Good-Friday the Petrobrusians once gathered a great multitude of their brethren, who brought with them all the crosses they could find, and that they made a large fire of them, on which they cooked meat, and gave it to the vast assemblage. This is told as an illustration of their blasphemous profanity. Their crucifixes, and along with them probably the images of the saints, were the idols they had been taught to worship, and when their eyes were opened they destroyed them, just as the converted heathen will now destroy their false gods.

(D) His preaching was with great power. He saw multitudes forsake the Roman Catholic Institution, get rebaptized, and follow Christ.

Peter's influence was very powerful, as the following quotation explains:

> Had the life of this illustrious man been spared, the Reformation probably would have occurred four hundred years earlier under Peter de Bruys instead of Martin Luther, and the Protestant nations of the earth would not only have had a deliverance from four centuries of priestly profligacy and widespread soul destruction, but they would have entered upon a godly life with a far more Scriptural creed than grand old Luther, still in a considerable measure wedded to Romish sacramentalism, was fitted to give them.

(William Cathcart, *Baptist Encyclopedia*)

(E) One of his friends was Henry of Lousanne, Switzerland, of Henrician fame.

(F) Peter de Bruys was eventually burned at St. Giles, two years prior to the death of Henry.

(G) After the death of these men, a cruel persecution arose against all who had followed their doctrine.

Historian Thieleman J. Van Braght in *Martyrs Mirror* or *Bloody Theatre of the Defenseless Christians* documented this:

> ...All manner of torment, fire, gallows, and cruel bloodshedding, yea so that the whole world was in commotion on account of it, yet could they not prevent this persuasion from spreading everywhere. And going forth into every country and kingdom, holding their worship secretly as well as openly....

(G) We see that many great men, some former religionists themselves, preached the Word of God boldly and saw many embrace the truth. This would be the case also with Arnold of Brescia.

2. The Arnoldists (A.D. 1135).
(A) Their leader was Arnold of Brescia.

    1. Arnold was an educated and talented man. He traveled to France early in life and studied under the renowned Peter Abelard. He left school, returned to Italy, and became a monk.

    2. Upon considering Scripture and witnessing the true evil of Roman Catholicism, Arnold began to spread the truth in the streets.

    3. He preached against sacramentalism and infant baptism and promoted adult faith and baptism.

    4. He immediately gained a following, who agreed with Arnold that the Roman church was apostate.

        a. Rome became alarmed; and in a council, he was condemned to perpetual silence. Arnold was then eventually excommunicated.

        b. Arnold fled Italy, and in the Swiss Canton of Zurich, he began his system of Scriptural reform.

        c. He returned to Rome full of zeal. A rebellion, coupled with revival, broke out.

d. For several years, successive popes could not stop this movement against Rome and back to the truth.

e. Finally, in A.D. 1155, Arnold was seized, crucified, and burnt. His ashes were scattered over the River Tiber.

f. Rome's feelings toward Arnold are expressed in the following quotation taken from the *New Advent Catholic Encyclopedia:*

"Forger of heresies," "sower of schisms," "enemy of the Catholic Faith," "schismatic," "heretic," such are the terms used by Otto of Freisingen, by the author of the "Historia Pontificalis," by the Abbot of Clairvaux, by Eugenius III, and Adrian IV to stigmatize Arnold."

(B) What caused Arnold to embrace Baptist principles?

1. The Bible.

a. It was in the Bible that Arnold learned of salvation by grace through faith.

Look up and read Ephesians 2:8-9. Do you remember when you, like Arnold, first discovered this truth?

b. It was in the Bible that Arnold learned of scriptural baptism.

Lesson Nine

Can you give Biblical reasons as to why baptism is by immersion and for believers only?

2. Excesses of the clergy.

a. Upon tragic circumstances of any sort, the common man was taught to regain God's favor by surrendering money and property to the clergy.

b. In short, the deeds of the Nicolaitans had again come to light.

Look up and read Revelation 2:6 and Revelation 2:15-16. Discuss the differences between these two passages.

3. Desecration of the church.

The historian Mosheim reported:

The festivals of fools and [donkeys] were established in most churches. On days of solemnity, they created a bishop of fools; and a [donkey] was led into the body of the church, dressed in a cape and four-cornered cap. When the people were dismissed, it was by the priests braying three times like a [donkey,] and the people responded in an asinine tone.

Please note that during this time in history many would die for the Word of God. The "Midnight of the Dark Ages" was well under way.

Review Questions

1. The _____ and _____ were twelfth-century people groups.

2. Many people were _____ with the _____ of Rome.

3. In this type of religious climate, when the pure Gospel was preached, everything from _____ to _____ broke out regularly.

4. History has not forgotten these two men and their _____.

5. Write out Psalm 145:4. "_____ _____ _____ _____."

6. Write a short paragraph explaining Psalm 145:4 in your own words.

_____
_____
_____
_____
_____

Lesson Nine

7. Peter de Bruys had a friend named _____ of Lousanne, Switzerland.

8. How did Peter de Bruys die? _____
_____

9. After Peter de Bruys and Henry died, what happened to their followers? _____
_____.

10. Who wrote *Martyrs Mirror*?
_____.

11. Arnold of Brescia studied under the renowned _____.

12. When Arnold returned to Italy, he became a _____.

13. Arnold saw firsthand the true _____ of Roman Catholicism.

14. Arnold was condemned to perpetual _____.

15. He preached against apostate Romanism until a rebellion, coupled with _____, broke out.

16. For several years, _____ _____ could not stop this movement.

17. How did Arnold die?

_____.

18. Give an example of Nicolaity during this period.

_____
_____
_____
_____
_____

Lesson Ten
The Picards, Lollards, and the Reformation
Part I

> Remember the days of old, consider the years of many generations: ask thy father, and he will shew thee; thy elders, and they will tell thee.
> **Deuteronomy 32:7**

Lesson ten spans the fourteenth through the sixteenth centuries. This lesson will amazingly stretch across Bohemia, England, Germany, and Switzerland. The continuing theme we have been concerned with will remain a major focus of this study. The groups in focus are the Picards and the Lollards. Their doctrine, preaching, leadership, devotion, and service will be briefly discussed. A great Baptist revival, unknown to most, will be given due attention.

In addition to our examination of these important Baptist landmarks, attention will be given to the Reformation. Aside from an understanding of the Dark Ages, the Reformation is one of the most important historical events that Baptists must understand.

Confusion abounds concerning the Reformation period. Many Baptists have been so misinformed by the Fundamentalist Movement and Reformed Christianity that they wrongly esteem the Reformation as something it was not. The author recently purchased a popular Christian video that was supposed to be a defense of the Bible. In this video, the narrator actually states that, "The day that Martin Luther nailed his ninety-five thesis on the church door in Wittenburg was our spiritual birthday." As you can imagine, anger gripped my soul as these words registered in my mind. This was saddening, but not shocking. Believe it or not, this type of undue veneration for Luther, Calvin, Zwingli, and the Reformation itself, has become commonplace among Baptists. We will present the true facts about these men and the Reformation. What the reader will be forced to do is to make a decision. Will we as a Baptist people continue to perpetuate lies to our children, or will we tell them the truth about the Reformation? It may mean admitting that you were wrong. True history doesn't lie. It is sometimes hard to accept, but it does not lie. For our generation to be helped by history, we must first accept the facts, even when other brethren do not!

Here are the facts.

Lesson Ten

Picards / Lollards (A.D. 1300)

1. The Picards.

(A) The Picards were simply Waldenses that migrated to Bohemia.

(B) They faced severe persecution.

(C) Heinrich Kramer, the German, Catholic inquisitor was given the full authority of the Pope to eradicate the Picards. He spent the last years of his life persecuting these innocent, Baptist Christians.

(D) They continued to preach with fervency.

(E) One of their converts was a man named Walter Lollard.

(F) Lollard became a Spirit-filled preacher.

His preaching brought revival all over the Rhine River region. People were affected by his preaching in Germany, Switzerland, Italy, and France. This revival reached the Waldenses and even the Albigenses, and his converts and the revival would eventually spill over into England. From here the Baptists would carry the Gospel across the ocean to North America.

If Baptists in America have anyone to thank today, it is not Luther or Calvin. It is definitely Walter Lollard.

1. His converts became known as Lollards.
2. The Picards were eventually tagged as Lollards.

The historian, Crosby, spoke of Lollard's time spent in Britain.

> In the time of Edward II, about the year 1315 Walter Lollard, a German Baptist preacher, a man of great renown among the Waldenses, came into England; he spread their doctrines very much in these parts, so that afterwards they went by the name Lollards.

3. God used Lollard to bring ancient Baptist Bible principles to Europe. These were the seeds of the Anabaptist movement.

Some Baptist historians have argued that there were many previous sightings of Baptist peoples and principles on English soil before Lollard made it there. We will not argue against this position. We will affirm, however, that Lollard's popularity among the brethren, and power to win the lost, made him a primary catapult of the Baptist faith in England. He was firmly grounded there, in the midst of the great revival. He and his followers scattered Gospel seeds that grew up into the English Anabaptists.

4. Walter Lollard, after returning from Wales, was caught and burned to death in Cologne in the year 1320.

Lollard's life and ministry are important pieces in the puzzle of Baptist perpetuity. Read and discuss the following point and especially the summary. These are extremely important!

His fellowship with the brethren in Wales authenticates the view that the Anabaptists of the European continent and the Isle of Britain share common roots, namely, the earthly ministry of the Lord Jesus Christ. The English Anabaptists practiced genuine, apostolic Christianity.

SUMMARY: Picards-Lollards

Walter Lollard was a Picard. The Picards were Waldenses that had migrated to Bohemia. The Waldenses are simply ancient Baptists. We established the fact that they are successors to the apostles.

So, we see the truth of the apostolic churches now, in history, reaches England through this revival. From England, the truth of God's Word and the branch of true Baptist churches traveled across the ocean to America. The Independent, separated Baptist churches in America are truly representative of the "Old Time Religion." Their origins can be traced through these Baptist groups all the way back to Jerusalem.

Do you understand the summary?

A Word on Baptist Succession: It is not necessary or even possible to trace the Baptists through physical records or existing, written history in an unbroken, church-by-church, chain-link succession. On the other hand, it certainly is encouraging to notice that an honest assessment of history proves that Baptist principles and Baptist people have existed in every century. Furthermore, the Baptist practice of churches planting churches would lead us to believe that there was a passing of the baton, even when we cannot trace it. These facts validate the author's position, which is that, our principles, which are held and defended by Baptists today, are ancient and originate with Jesus Christ. A careful comparison of the basic doctrines of twenty-first century Independent Baptists, with the Bible, bears this out beyond argument!

The Reformation

1. What was it?

The Reformation was an attempt to reform the Roman Catholic Church. It began in the early fifteen hundreds and lasted several years. It produced many new and different forms of church government. More than a few "denominations" of religion exist today as a result of it. The results of the Reformation, when lined up with Scripture, do not

Lesson Ten

fare well. Aside from this, the Reformation accomplished many other not so praiseworthy feats. Sadly, none of these accomplishments were a true reformation of Roman Catholicism. Roman Catholicism is just as corrupt in doctrine and practice as it has ever been. In addition, the churches created from this event have become so liberal, that they are not a whit better than the institution they were trying to reform. It has been often stated that "all of Rome's little babies went back to momma." Remember, when something starts unscriptural, it usually ends unscriptural. One might say that the "Great" Reformation was greatly overrated!

Phillip Schaff may have stated it best when he wrote the following:

> The Reformation everywhere had its defects and sins, which it is impossible to justify. How cruel was the persecution of the Anabaptists, who by no means were only revolutionary fanatics but for the most part simple, honest Christians and suffered and died for liberty of conscience and the separation of church and state. And how sad were the moral state and the rude theological quarrels in Germany. No wonder that Melanchthon longed for deliverance from the rabies theologorum. I hope God has something better and greater in store for His Church than the Reformation.

Some wrongly state that Luther brought back to the church the lost doctrine of justification by faith. To what degree Luther embraced faith alone is questionable, based on his defense of infant baptism. Secondly, Romanism is not "the church." In addition to this, Luther could not have restored something that was never lost. Had Luther simply searched the local wilderness he would have found Baptists preaching this great truth of the Bible, as they had done in every age. The Catholic Institution never once embraced faith alone for salvation. How can something be restored to an institution that never had it? The Protestants simply stumbled upon a truth that the Baptists had faithfully perpetuated for 1500 years.

Luther believed in infant baptism, as did the vast majority of Reformers. Please read and discuss the following quotes:

> a. In Luther's *Catechism*, p. 173, #251, he states: "How do you prove that infants, too, are to be baptized?" Then he continues, "Infants, too, are to be baptized—because they are included in the words- 'all nations.'"

> b. In his *Small Catechism*, p. 173, under B, he said the following: "Because Holy Baptism is the only means whereby infants, who, too, must

be born again, can ordinarily be regenerated and brought to faith."

c. The following are words that Luther had confirmed: *Article IX: Of Baptism.* "Of Baptism they teach that it is necessary to salvation, and that through Baptism is offered the grace of God, and that children are to be baptized who, being offered to God through Baptism are received into God's grace. They condemn the Anabaptists, who reject the baptism of children."
Source: (*The Confession of Faith: Which Was Submitted to His Imperial Majesty Charles V, at the Diet of Augsburg in the Year 1530,* by Philip Melanchthon, 1497-1560, translated by F. Bente and W. H. T. Dau. Published in: *Triglot Concordia: The Symbolical Books of the Ev. Lutheran Church.* St. Louis: Concordia Publishing House, 1921, pp. 37-95.)

d. Ulrich Zwingli, the Swiss reformer, is a man who is wrongly venerated by some Fundamentalists. He clearly lets everyone know his position on Baptist immersion when he states:
"Drown the Dippers." (Davis, Tamar. *A General History of the Sabbatarian Churches,* 1851; Reprinted 1995 by Commonwealth Publishing, Salt Lake City, p. 106).

e. John Calvin was baptized as an infant in the Roman Catholic Institution. Although he repudiated some of Rome's errors, he never repudiated his baptism. Notice the following:
"Calvin said of his baptism (in the Roman church): I renounce the charism, but not the baptism." Charism is sprinkling oil. (*History of the Christian Church*, Phillip Schaff.)

f. A careful study of *The Works of John Knox* reveals an animosity towards Anabaptism. Richard Kyle gives the following assessment: "Were all who were baptized in league with God and therefore elect? Knox does not address this enigmatic question. On one hand, his statements in his baptismal tract-if taken literally-would seem to indicate such a course of action." Richard G. Kyle is Professor of History and Religion at Tabor College (Hillsboro, KS). John Knox, *The Works of John Knox*, ed. David Laing, 6 Vols. (Edinburgh: Printed for the Bannatyne Club, 1846-64).

2. How did the Reformation begin?

The Reformation began on October 31, 1517, when German monk Martin Luther nailed his 95 Theses to the Castle Church door in Wittenberg, Germany. He was disgruntled over the sale of in-

Lesson Ten

dulgences, unscriptural teachings, and the overall corruption of his church. These issues caused him to publicly denounce the Catholic church and the Pope. He exposed Rome, both with his preaching as well as his writings. Luther wrote a book entitled *The Babylonian Captivity of the Congregation*. In his book he explained that the end of the Babylonian captivity of the Jews in 457 B.C. started the 490 years countdown to the first coming of the Messiah. Luther further taught that the end of the Babylonian captivity of the congregation in 1517 started the countdown to the second coming of Christ. This congregation, of course, was composed of his newly rescued followers. Luther showed an uncanny bravery when dealing with the Roman Catholic authorities. While appearing before Emperor Charles V to answer for his writings, he boldly stated:

> I cannot submit my faith either to the Pope or to the Councils, because it is clear as day that they have frequently erred and contradicted each other. Unless therefore, I am convinced by the testimony of Scripture...I cannot and will not retract...Here I stand, I can do no other. So help me God, Amen.

It was in this type of spirit that the Reformation began!

Review Questions

1. This lesson deals with two Baptist groups. They are the _____ and the _____.

2. The Picards were _____ that migrated from _____.

3. _____ _____ was a convert to the Picards and became a great leader and preacher.

4. The preaching of Walter Lollard brought revival all over the _____ _____ region.

5. This revival spilled over into _____.

6. Because of the great leadership of Lollard among the Picards, his converts became known as the _____.

7. The Anabaptists of the European _____ and the Isle of _____ share common _____.

Lesson Ten

8. It is impossible to trace the Baptists through physical records in an unbroken _____-link succession.

9. Our principles are _____ and originate with _____ _____.

10. The Reformation was an attempt to reform the _____ _____ Church.

11. One might say that the "Great" Reformation was _____ _____.

12. Had Luther searched the local wilderness he would have found _____ preaching justification by faith.

13. Luther believed in infant _____.

14. Ulrich Zwingli once said, "Drown the _____."

15. John Calvin never _____ his Catholic baptism.

16. John Knox tied election to the ordinance of _____.

17. The Reformation began on October 31, _____.

18. Martin Luther nailed his ____ _____ to the _____ _____ door in _____, Germany.

19. Luther stated, "I cannot submit my faith either to the _____ or to the _____."

20. Write out Deuteronomy 32:7. "_____."

LESSON ELEVEN
The Reformation Part II
The Anabaptists Part I

> And when he had opened the fifth seal, I saw under the altar the souls of them that were slain for the word of God, and for the testimony which they held:
>
> **Revelation 6:9**

Lesson eleven is a continuation of the study of the Reformation. As you have already noticed, the position of the author is not the popular position of many of our Baptist brethren. This is not because Baptists are willingly attempting to make the Reformers and their movement something it was not. The popular views of the Reformation are almost entirely the result of the ignorance of Baptists concerning legitimate history. Those who hold to the idea that the Reformers and their movement was a great blessing to mankind, and that it had no problems, are simply repeating the Protestant view of this event. The Fundamentalist Movement of the twentieth century has been so friendly to Protestantism, that many Baptists have used history books written and promoted by the Protestants themselves. At the same time, most Baptists have never consulted the histories of J.T. Christian, Thomas Armitage, Graves, or Shackleford!

The great error of infant baptism, which was held to by the Reformers, has already been documented as a part of this study. The present lesson will show the reader very plain proof that these Reformers were murderous villains! The author's disdain for the "Reformation" will be understood by the reader by the time this lesson is through. For those who doubt the validity of these truths, I have somewhat to say. In my possession is a disc by the publisher, Baptist Standard Bearer. On this disc are over one hundred trustworthy, and scholarly, histories of the Baptists. The documentation, on the evils of the Reformers contained in this one disc, numbers in the hundreds of pages. In this lesson we will offer just a minute sampling of all that is available to bear out these truths.

The second half of the present lesson will introduce an amazing body of believers, the Anabaptists. Much could be said here of this Godly company. We will, however, forgo introductions in order to get to the exciting facts. The Anabaptists carried the torch of truth across the ocean to these United States of America. Every Baptist ought to know some facts about these baptized believers!

Lesson Eleven

Reformation Part II

1. The positive results of the Reformation.

(A) Martin Luther translated the Bible into German. Soon all the countries of Europe followed his example by translating the Scriptures into their languages. There was a revival in boldness that swept across Europe. Many people would be able to personally examine the Scriptures for the first time in history. The printing press, still a somewhat recent invention, began to be a vital tool in spreading the Word of God to the lost. The author feels more comfortable giving credit to the Lord and the Word of God for the many that were saved during this timeframe. Luther's confusing message of faith plus a necessary infant baptism cannot be credited with a Biblical revival. On the other hand, it was through Luther's boldness that the Word of God began to be printed and distributed more than at any other time in history up to this point. As people read the Bible for themselves, the Word of God wrought conviction unto salvation.

Today, the church that Luther founded still carries the same confusing message as it always has. They claim that salvation is by faith on the one hand; but on the other hand, they preach the damnable heresy of a necessary infant baptism. Rarely are people saved under such confusion. The author had an opportunity, while doing his undergraduate work, of working in a mental home that was owned and operated by the Lutherans. In the mornings all of the residents were carted off to chapel. Be assured that the message there was a confusing mix of universal salvation to all, secured through the baptismal rite. Never once was a clear presentation of the Gospel given.

(B) Roman Catholicism was dealt a serious blow. Upon Luther publicly exposing some of the major problems with Catholicism, multitudes forsook their parish and began to meet with unapproved congregations. There were great masses that no longer wanted to be under Catholic authority. This was more of a mass exodus than it was a reformation. In Germany, Switzerland, England, and all over Europe, men began to question or outright rebel against the Catholic institution. This was good. Luther, Zwingli, and Calvin did not have a pure Gospel; but they did influence people to leave Romanism. Whenever anyone leaves Romanism, it is a positive thing. One step away from works, for a searching heart, is one step closer to the truth.

2. Negative Results of the Reformation.

(A) Baptist Persecution. One of the greatest lies that has ever been perpetuated is the idea that somehow the Reformation was liberating for the already persecuted Baptists. This is far from the truth. Because Martin Luther was trained in the Augustinian theological system, a simple discovery of the role of faith would not undo his warped worldview. Luther was a dominion theologian. Even though he separated from the Catholic institution, the Catholic ideals of world conquest and dominion on behalf of God did not change in his mind. Because of this, he was a persecutor of our forefathers. This would be the case with other prominent Reformation leaders. Zwingli and Calvin were also of this viewpoint. Instead of the Reformation being liberating for the Baptists, it was detrimental to Baptist liberty. The Reformation caused it to be open season on the Baptists. Their enemies were multiplied from Roman persecution alone, to persecution by Rome, as well as by several Reformation groups.

1. William Pettingill wrote a helpful treatise concerning Protestant persecution of Baptists, in *A Hangover from Rome*:

> When the Reformation came, these Anabaptists or Antipedobaptists did all they could to help the Reformers; but when the Reformers came into power they turned against the Anabaptists and persecuted them as Rome had done and continued to do; and thus the troubles of the Anabaptists were increased instead of diminished, for now they had persecutors on both sides - from Romanism on one hand and

from Protestantism on the other.

All honor to the great Reformers, but the truth must be told that in their reform they brought with them out of Rome the two hateful errors, union of church and state and infant baptism; and moreover when they had the power in their hands because of this union of church and state, they themselves became popes in their own realm and persecuted those who would not conform to their ways. The Lutheran church became the established church of Germany, and persecuted the Anabaptists for nonconformity. While Zwingli held power in Switzerland the Senate passed a law making infant baptism compulsory and providing that 'if any presume to rebaptize those who were baptized before, they should be drowned,' and at Vienna many Anabaptists were so tied together in chains that one drew the other after him into the river, wherein they were all suffocated. Calvin in his field, Cromwell in England, Knox in Scotland - these all stuck to the union of church and state and infant baptism, and used their power, when they had power, to seek to force others to conform with their own views.

2. Michael Servetus was burned at the stake in Geneva by John Calvin on October 27, 1553. In Stephan Zweig's book, *Erasmus: The Right to Heresy*, the following is documented:

The chains attached to the stake were wrapped four

or five times around the poor wretch's wasted body... The executioner kindled the faggots and the murder began. When the flames rose around him, Servetus uttered a dreadful cry...Jesus, son of the everlasting God have pity on me. The struggle with death lasted half an hour. The flames abated, the smoke dispersed, and attached to the blackened stake there remained, above the glowing embers, a black sickening, charred mass, a loathsome jelly, which had lost human semblance.

3. From *Hunted Heretic* by R. H. Bainton, we glean the following:

As Servetus screamed his way into eternity, Dr. John Calvin, 'The greatest light in the world,' was behind the doors of his study; he did not smell the odious, sickening stench of human flesh burned to an horrible pulp. The next Sunday this hypocrite, the famed theologian...went to church. Clad in his standard black cassock, he entered the pulpit and struggled to justify his dastardly deed before a vast congregation who sat cold, stunned, and fearfully silent.

4. Limited space will not allow for a thorough discussion of the thousands of non-conformists persecuted by the Reformers. This subject will be revisited again in our discussion of the English Anabaptists.

(B) False doctrine produced by the Reformers has caused much confusion. Baptists throughout the years have been inundated with Protestant-based challenges to their doctrine. Can you name any Protestant doctrines that Baptists have had to deal with and refute?

Was Martin Luther a born-again believer?

The question has often been asked, "Was Martin Luther saved?" The author has a strong opinion about Luther based on many hours of research and general reading. This opinion will not be presented here. However, let the reader ponder the following facts in order to form his own opinion.

> 1. Luther had an experience in which he discovered that "the just shall live by faith."
> 2. Luther left dead religion and started his own state-church.
> 3. Luther held to infant baptism until his death.
> 4. Luther cruelly persecuted the church of the Lord Jesus Christ until his death.

Contrast the above facts with the life of the Apostle Paul.

> 1. Paul fell down in repentance and faith and was heartily converted.

Lesson Eleven

2. Paul left dead religion and joined up with a true church.
3. Paul was beaten repeatedly for standing against false doctrine, including false views of baptism.
4. Paul quit persecuting the church of the Lord Jesus Christ the day he became a Christian.

These are the basic facts. Now, you decide if you believe Luther was saved.

Truly these issues are best left to the Lord.

Anabaptists (of Europe and Great Britain) - Part I (1310?-1635)

1. The name means "Re-baptizer."

(A) The name is derived from the fact that all those saved out of apostate churches must submit to scriptural baptism.

(B) This is not the beginnings of a new group. The author believes that every group that has been examined in this study was under attack for the same stand, and therefore all groups were probably called this slanderous term (Anabaptist).

(C) This group certainly espoused the same basic set of doctrinal beliefs as the previous Baptist groups we have examined.

(D) Other popular names used for this group

were:
- Neodonatists & Paulicians. These terms related them back to the Paulicians and Donatists of the previous 10 centuries.
- Catabaptists- Meaning "down-dippers."
- Staff Carriers. Their pastors were identified by their practice of carrying canes or staffs, in contrast to the sword and bishop's crook held by the clergy of establishment churches.
- Cathari, Sacramentarians, Winklers, and Communists were some of the many slanderous names used by the enemies of God to describe these good people.

(E) These believers were migrated Waldenses, Lollards, Albigenses, and Welsh Baptists.
Note of interest: Bible translator William Tyndale (1530's) had Welsh Baptist roots. His parents were Welsh Baptists and resided in southern Wales.
(F) They were despised by all as were their forefathers.

A recommended field trip for the student of Baptist history is to the Menno-Hof museum in Shipshewana, Indiana. (The Independent Baptists and the Mennonites share a common heritage.) There are both reproductions of the rack, which was used for cruel torture, as well as the metal cattle catcher,

Lesson Eleven

called the "Anabaptist catcher." It is very eye-opening for the student to realize that these are not just stories but not-so-long-ago realities!

Review Questions

1. The popular views of the Reformation are almost entirely the _____ of the _____ of _____ concerning real, legitimate history.

2. Many Baptists have used history books written and promoted by the _____.

3. These Reformers were _____ villains.

4. The _____ carried the torch of truth across the ocean to these United States of America.

5. Martin Luther _____ the _____ into German.

6. Many people would be able to personally examine the _____ for the first time.

7. Luther preached faith plus a necessary _____ baptism.

8. Roman Catholicism was dealt a _____ _____.

9. Martin Luther was trained in the _____ theological system.

10. Luther was a dominion _____.

11. Instead of the Reformation being liberating for the Baptists, it was _____ to _____ _____.

12. When the Reformation came, the Anabaptists did all they could to _____ the Reformers.

13. The Lutheran church became the established church of _____ and _____ the _____.

14. _____ _____ was burned at the stake by John Calvin.

15. As Servetus screamed his way into eternity, Calvin was in his _____.

Lesson Eleven

16. _____ _____ produced by the Reformers has caused much confusion.

17. The name Anabaptist means "_____ _____."

18. The Anabaptists were migrated _____, _____, _____, and _____ _____.

19. Bible translator _____ _____ had _____ _____ roots.

20. The _____ was used for cruel torture and the metal cattle catcher was called the "_____ _____."

LESSON TWELVE
The Anabaptists Part II

> And these all, having obtained a good report through faith...
>
> **Hebrews 11:39a**

Lesson twelve is a continuation of our study on Anabaptism. The name, Anabaptists is used simply as an identifying tool. This is the name for the body of true believers in Switzerland, Wales, and England from the thirteenth through the fifteenth centuries. We do not agree with the implication made when the enemies of truth maliciously use this tag. We know that our brethren who inhabited the previously mentioned regions never did "rebaptize" anyone. Not one believer was ever rebaptized by our forefathers. Our Baptist forebears simply administered the scriptural ordinance to all who met the Biblical qualifications. If this meant immersing someone who had previously been involved in an unscriptural ceremony put on by an unscriptural body, then the Baptists never hesitated to do so. For this reason alone, Baptists were charged with unnecessarily rebaptizing those who had been baptized before. The Catholics and the Reformers took great offense at the idea that Baptists took no note of their false baptisms. Thomas Armitage, one of the great, classic, Baptist historians once made the following observation:

> A word here may be necessary as to the proper name of this interesting people; were they Baptists or Anabaptists? They are commonly characterized as 'Anabaptists' by friends and foes; yet this name was especially offensive to them, as it charged them with rebaptizing those whom they regarded as unbaptized and because it was intended as a stigma. By custom their most friendly historians call them 'Anabaptists,' yet many of their candid opponents speak of them as 'Baptists.' The Petrobrussians complained that Peter of Clugny 'slandered' them by calling them 'Anabaptists,' so did their Swiss and German brethren after them. The London Confession, 1646, protests that the English Baptists were 'commonly though unjustly called Anabaptists.' Knollys resented this name, calling it 'scandalous;' and Haggar, 1653, rebukes Baxter for its use. 'You do very wickedly to call them Anabaptists, thereby to cast odium upon us... why, I pray you, are you so wicked and malicious as to call them Anabaptists?' Black-wood, 1645, complains of being 'nicknamed Anabaptists. We deny your title; Ana-baptism signifies baptism again; our consciences are fully satisfied with one baptism, provided it be such as we judge to be the baptism of Christ; and if our consciences judge that sprinkling we had in our infancy to be none of Christ's baptism, I ask you whether can we, in good conscience, rest satisfied

Lesson Twelve

> therewith? We are, if we must needs be new named, Antipedobaptists, or Catapedobaptists, but no Anabaptists.' Baptists now refuse to be called 'Anabaptists,' and for the same reasons. Respect for ourselves and our ancestry demands that the offensive title be thrown aside...
>
> (*A History of the Baptists* - Volume 1, Thomas Armitage, 1886, Baptist Standard Bearer.)

The above quote explains our rejection of this name and its underlying notions; however, the name is used in such a study as this to clarify the group referenced here as the "Anabaptists Proper" of Europe, because this is the name history knows them by.

Scriptural Baptism

It is needful at this time to interject an important lesson concerning baptism. What makes baptism legitimate? What makes baptism illegitimate? These are questions that demand Biblical answers. The following points are truths that our Baptist forefathers were willing to die for. First, it is important to mention that legitimate baptism must have a saved individual as its subject. The Bible knows of no one being baptized until after they have believed with all their heart (Acts 8). The next issue is authority. Christ committed the ordinances to one institution, the local church. This is the only institution that can administer baptism with the approval of Jesus Christ. The man administering the baptism must have the authority of Christ, through His church. Furthermore, the hands that baptize must be the hands of a child of God. No lost man has any part in the holy ordinances of Christ and of God. The mode of baptism is also of utmost importance. Our Lord went down into the water and came up out of the water when He was baptized by John the Baptist. John baptized in the river Jordan. The eunich in Acts 8 went to where there was much water. Complete immersion into water is the only baptism that is biblical baptism. That is to say that the idea of different modes of baptism is an invention of wicked men. There really is no such thing as "modes of baptism."

One might say, "He is a good brother who simply allows for different modes of baptism." This was the case in a popular Baptist college. A Presbyterian, baby sprinkler was a guest speaker in this particular school. This was defended by some who pointed to his stand on the King James Bible as a way to justify his unscriptural practices concerning baptism. How ironic that some would defend a man's unscriptural practice by pointing out his defense of the Bible. Are not those that defend the Bible the most responsible to live the Bible? It is vitally important that Baptist, Bible believers understand that pouring is not baptism at all. Sprinkling is not baptism. For that matter, getting sprayed with a garden hose in the back yard is not baptism. The baptism committed to us by our Lord is immersion. This baptism is the only one that testifies of Christ's death, burial, and resurrection. This is the only one found in the Bible. The issue of mode is so very important because if it is not right, the whole purpose for baptism is destroyed. Again, that purpose is to picture publicly Christ's death, burial, and resurrection. The truth is that those men who pour and sprinkle are not baptizing their converts at all. How sad it is to be a new, child of God and to be kept from your very first step of obedience by a so-called minister! We must contend for this truth. If our mode becomes corrupt, our ordinance becomes corrupt. Whenever the ordinances have been corrupted or minimized in history, the Gospel, itself, was corrupted not long after.

The final part of scriptural baptism, as understood and defended by Baptists throughout the ages, is that it must be done in the name of the Father, and the Son, and the Holy Ghost (Matt 28).

Anything that does not meet these five criteria is not baptism. It may be impressive, it may be done by a "good" man, it may be accepted by "the brethren," but scriptural, Baptist baptism is just that-scriptural!

It was over these points of doctrine that the Baptists were burned at the stake not so long ago!

The Anabaptists Part II

1. Notable Anabaptist leaders.

(A) Conrad Grebel. He was a fiery defender of the Baptist position. He is often referred to as the "Father of the Anabaptists."

1. He baptized George Blaurock, a converted Catholic priest, on January 21, 1525, at the home of Felix Mans.
2. Zwingli considered Grebel a great threat in Zurich, Switzerland, as Conrad Grebel debated him on the Mass and over baptism.
3. In January of 1525, Zwingli won a public dispute, and the council mandated infant baptism within eight days. The council demanded Grebel and Mans desist from debating with Zwingli. At this point, they gathered in the home of Mans, and Blaurock was baptized.
4. He also baptized Wolfgang Ulimann, a former monk.
5. He was arrested and sentenced to life in prison, but Grebel escaped with the help of friends.
6. Grebel died of the plague in March of 1526. By the time of his death, he had participated in as many as 500 baptisms, according to some sources.

(B) George Blaurock. An ex-monk and powerful preacher.
   1. He was the first man Grebel ever baptized.
   2. Some say he was the first adult baptized in Zurich; however, this is highly unlikely. To accept this would mean to believe that the true faith had never been preached and practiced in Zurich from the time of Christ.
   3. He baptized thousands of converts during his ministry.
   4. Cathcart reports on page 71, of Volume 1, in his *Baptist Encyclopedia*, the following:

> Grebel, Manz, Hubmaier, and Blaurock were imprisoned and banished. Manz was finally drowned. Though continually harassed, these noble witnesses for Christ were very active, traveling from place to place, preaching at night in private houses to the people, who were anxious to hear. Some preachers baptized hundreds, if not thousands, of persons. From Zurich they spread throughout Switzerland, southern Germany, the Netherlands, Moravia, etc.

   5. George Blaurock was burned at the stake in 1529.

(C) Balthaser Hubmaier. He was a very learned man and an expert in theology, who left Lu-

theranism and embraced the Baptist position.

1. J. T. Christian stated that this man was "The great apostle of the Baptists of Moravia."
2. He pastored in Switzerland, where he left under threat of death. He made it to Zurich but was there captured and tortured for over six months.
3. Upon his release, he traveled to Moravia where he published sixteen books.
4. It is said that his ministry there produced over 6,000 baptized converts.
5. He was burned at the stake in 1528. Three days later, his wife met her end in the bottom of the Danube River, as she was drowned.

(D) Felix Manz. A highly acclaimed Hebrew scholar who debated with Zwingli and the authorities of Zurich over baptism.

1. Historian Verduin reports of Manz:

> He was placed in a rowboat with his wrists firmly tied together and passed over his cocked

Lesson Twelve

knees, and a heavy piece of wood thrust between his bent knees and his elbows. Trussed up in this manner-making swimming impossible-he was rowed to the other side of the Limmat River, then thrown overboard.

    2. He died a martyr's death in 1527.

(E) Michael Sattler. He was an Anabaptist from Germany, one of the first German Anabaptists to be martyred.

    1. Verduin records his death sentence as such:

Michael is to be committed to the executioner, who is to take him to the city square and there cut out his tongue. Then he is to tie him to a wagon and with a red-hot pair of blacksmith tongs tear shreds of flesh from his body, doing so five times more on the way to the fire. He is to burn his body to powder, as an archheretic.

    2. Sattler died a martyr's death in 1527.

(F) Menno Simons. Known as the leader of the "Quiet Anabaptists."

    1. While attending the execution of an Anabaptist in 1531, this Dutch Roman Catholic priest

fell under conviction and, not long after, was saved and became a Baptist.

2. He was a great leader for a time.

3. On page 91 of J.M. Cramp's *Baptist History*, he wrote:

> Menno Simon and other laborers in the cause introduced 'great multitudes' to the churches. The spirit of reform must have taken fast hold of the minds of the people, or they would not have embraced so readily a system, the profession of which was a sure passport to persecution in its most painful and revolting forms. Luther and his coadjutors opened the door of the temple of freedom to others, but remained themselves in the porch. They feared to penetrate into the interior. The Baptists passed by them, entered in, and explored the recesses of the hallowed place.

4. Sadly, doctrinal errors began to surface.
    (a) He advocated pacificism.
        He advocated not holding public office for any reason.
        He did not believe in bearing arms.
        He did not believe in capital punishment.
    (b) He taught that Christ got His humanity in Heaven, not from Mary.

Note of interest: As with many false cults in our

present day, the modern-day Mennonite movement only slightly resembles the teachings of their self-adopted founder.

(G) Everyone persecuted the Anabaptists. It was open season in England and elsewhere.
    1. Luther, Zwingli, and Calvin were all persecutors of the Baptists.
    2. Bloody Mary took the English throne in 1553 and murdered and exiled thousands.

(H) It was their stand for Baptist principles, such as baptism and liberty of conscience, which would perpetuate the Gospel until it would land in North America! Baptists today ought to appreciate the lives and labors of these great people!

Review Questions

1. The name Anabaptists is used simply as an _____ _____.

2. The Anabaptists were the true believers from the _____ through the _____ centuries.

3. The Baptists never did "_____" anyone.

4. We use the name Anabaptists because this is the name _____ knows them by.

5. Christ committed the ordinances to _____ institution, the _____ _____.

6. The hands that baptize must be the hands of a _____ _____ _____.

7. The _____ of baptism is of utmost importance.

8. Complete _____ _____ is the only baptism that is Biblical baptism.

9. The idea of different _____ of baptism is the invention of wicked men.

10. Immersion is the only type of baptism that testifies of Christ's _____, _____, and _____.

11. If the ordinances become corrupted, the _____ will become corrupted.

Lesson Twelve

12. Many _____ were burned at the stake over baptism.

13. Conrad _____ is often referred to as the _____ of the _____.

14. George _____ baptized _____ of converts during his ministry.

15. _____ _____ was burned at the stake in _____.

16. _____ _____ was called "The great apostle of the Baptists of Moravia."

17. Hubmaier's ministry in Moravia produced over _____ baptized converts.

18. _____ _____ was drowned in the Limmat River in 1527.

19. _____ _____ was burned to powder in 1527.

20. _____ _____ was known as the leader of the quiet Anabaptists.

21. For a time Menno Simons was a _____ leader.

22. _____ persecuted the Anabaptists.

23. _____ Mary murdered and exiled thousands of Anabaptists.

Lesson Twelve

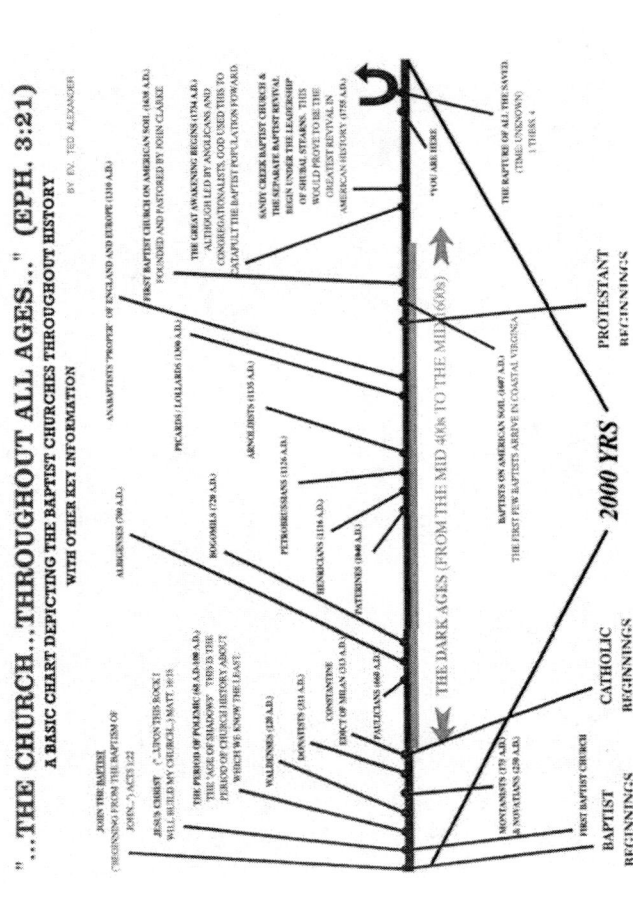

Answer Key

Lesson One
1. STONES
2. FORGET
3. GENERATION
4. DENY
5. STIRS
6. MARTYRS
7. PERSECUTION
8. CHURCHES
9. 11
10. INDIFFERENT
11. YES
12. 1851

Lesson Two
1. DOZEN
2. BEGAN
3. THE PURITANS
4. SEPARATE
5. BILL OF RIGHTS
6. CALVINISTIC
7. BAPTIST HISTORY
8. 100
9. FUNDAMENTALIST
    PROTESTANT
10. 1900
11. HEROES
    FATHERS

12. GOD
    CHILDREN

Lesson Three
1. ORIGIN
2. WORD
3. SCHOLARLY HISTORY
4. CATHOLIC
   REFORMATION
5. SEPARATION
6. ORIGINAL
7. CATHOLIC
8. GOD
9. JESUS
10. APOSTLES
11. CHURCH
12. PENTECOST
13. GOD
14. BAPTIST
    CATHOLICS
    PROTESTANTS

Lesson Four
1. LOCAL CHURCH
2. BAPTIZERS
   BAPTISTS
3. APOSTATE BAPTISM
4. APOSTLES
5. PROVEN
6. MODERN
7. CHRISTIAN

Answer Key

8. VALLEYS
   ALPS
9. MONTHS
10. MILLION
11. ITALIC
    OLIVETAN
12. TESTAMENT
13. PEDDLERS

Lesson Five
1. NOVATIANS
   MONATISTS
2. MANIFOLD
3. MONTANUS
4. RITUALISM
   NICOLAITY
   LAXNESS
5. JEZEBEL
6. INTERPRET
7. DISCIPLINE
8. CONSCIENCE
   UNBELIEF
9. TERTULLIAN
10. NOVATIAN
11. PURITY OF CHURCH MEMBERSHIP
    RIGID CHURCH DISCIPLINE
    REBAPTISM OF APOSTATES
    SCRIPTURAL BAPTISM
12. BY IMMERSION
    FOR MATURE ADULTS
    WITHOUT GREAT CEREMONY
    ON CHURCH AUTHORITY

13. YES
14. FRANCE
15. SIXTH
16. 1) STRONG ON CHURCH MEMBERSHIP AND COMMITMENT
    2) STRONG ON POST CONVERSION IMMERSION
    3) STRONG ON SOUL LIBERTY
    4) STRONG AGAINST ECCLESIASTICAL HIERARCHIES

Lesson Six
PAGE 64: THE BAPTISTS CATHOLICISM

1. BLOODY
   SORROWFUL
2. EXTINCTO NOMINEE CHRISTORIUM
3. CHRISTIANITY
   EXTINCT
4. IMPERIAL
5. MANY ANSWERS ARE ACCEPTABLE. BASICALLY WE WANT TO REMEMBER THAT GOD IS IN CONTROL.
6. ORDINATION
7. NOVATIANS
8. REBAPTIZED
9. CONSTANTINE
10. MILAN
11. 17
    ROMAN
12. WOMAN

Answer Key

    SEVEN MOUNTAINS
13. BLOOD
    SAINTS
    MARTYRS
14. THEY USED PAULINE NAMES FOR THEIR LEADERS
    THEY EMPHASIZED THE PAULINE EPISTLES
15. FIRST
    BRANCH
    ANTIOCHAN
16. TARGET
    CHEST
17. THEODORA
    MICHAEL III
    100,000

Lesson Seven
1. ALBIGENSES
2. ALBI
3. WALDENSES
4. ECCLESIASTICAL
5. MANICHAEANS
6. ONE OF THE BLACK SPOTS IN HISTORY
7. DOMINICANS
8. FRANCISCANS
   JESUITS
9. EXTERMINATE
10. 60,000
11. SEVERAL HUNDRED THOUSAND
12. EXTERMINATED

13. BOGOMILISM
14. DARK AGES
15. SIMPLY A TIME WHEN NO GREAT INVENTIONS CAME FORTH.
    NOR WAS IT JUST A PERIOD IN WHICH NO GREAT MUSIC WAS COMPOSED AND NOT GREAT ART PAINTED.
16. AUGUSTINE
17. DOMINION
18. THE HORRIBLE TIMEFRAME IN HISTORY THAT SPANNED OVER A THOUSAND YEARS (INCLUDING THE MIDDLE AGES, THIS TIMEFRAME BEGAN AROUND 400 AND LASTED INTO THE SIXTEENTH CENTURY). DURING THESE DARK CENTURIES THE BIBLE WAS THE FORBIDDEN BOOK. ALL DISSENT WAS PUNISHABLE BY TORTURE, BANISHMENT, DISMEMBERMENT, BURNING, AND A HOST OF OTHER CRUELTIES. THE WHOLE EUROPEAN CONTINENT WAS DOMINATED BY THE ROMAN CATHOLIC EMPIRE.

Lesson Eight
1. BOGOMILS
   PATERINES
   HENRICIANS
2. MIDNIGHT
   DARK
3. PORNOCRACY
4. LIBERTY

5. SPIRIT
   WORD
6. BOGOMILS
7. BALKAN
8. FRIENDS
   GOD
9. INNOCENT III
10. PERSONAL SEPARATION
11. THE ABOMINATION OF DESOLATION STANDING IN THE HOLY PLACE
12. CRUCIFIX
13. LOUSANNE, SWITZERLAND
    BENEDICTINE MONK
14. REVIVAL BROKE OUT IN MANS AND IN OTHER CITIES
15. REPENTED
    MARRY THEM
16. STARVATION

Lesson Nine
1. PETROBRUSSIANS
   ARNOLDISTS
2. DISGRUNTLED
   HYPOCRISY
3. RIOTS
   REVIVALS
4. INFLUENCE
5. ONE GENERATION SHALL PRAISE THY WORKS TO ANOTHER, AND SHALL DECLARE THY MIGHTY ACTS.
6. ANSWER SHOULD REFLECT THIS THOUGHT - OUR GENERATION IS RE-

SPONSIBLE BEFORE GOD TO SHARE OUR HERITAGE WITH THE NEXT GENERATION.
7. HENRY
8. BURNED AT THE STAKE
9. THEY WERE PERSECUTED
10. THIELEMAN J. VAN BRAGHT
11. PETER ABELARD
12. MONK
13. EVIL
14. SILENCE
15. REVIVAL
16. SUCCESSIVE POPES
17. CRUCIFIXION AND BURNING
18. UPON TRAGIC CIRCUMSTANCES OF ANY SORT, THE COMMON MAN WAS TAUGHT TO REGAIN GOD'S FAVOR BY SURRENDERING MONEY AND PROPERTY TO THE CLERGY.

Lesson Ten
1. PICARDS
   LOLLARDS
2. WALDENSES
   BOHEMIA
3. WALTER LOLLARD
4. RHINE RIVER
5. ENGLAND
6. LOLLARDS
7. CONTINENT
   BRITAIN
   ROOTS

ANSWER KEY

8. CHAIN
9. ANCIENT
   JESUS CHRIST
10. ROMAN CATHOLIC
11. GREATLY OVERRATED
12. BAPTISTS
13. BAPTISM
14. DIPPERS
15. REJECTED
16. BAPTISM
17. 1517
18. 95 THESES
    CASTLE CHURCH
    WITTENBURG
19. POPE
    COUNCILS
20. REMEMBER THE DAYS OF OLD, CONSIDER THE YEARS OF MANY GENERATIONS: ASK THY FATHER, AND HE WILL SHEW THEE; THY ELDERS, AND THEY WILL TELL THEE."

Lesson Eleven
1. RESULT
   IGNORANCE
   BAPTISTS
2. PROTESTANTS
3. MURDEROUS
4. ANABAPTISTS
5. TRANSLATED
   BIBLE
6. SCRIPTURES

7. INFANT
8. SERIOUS BLOW
9. AUGUSTINIAN
10. THEOLOGIAN
11. DETRIMENTAL
    BAPTIST LIBERTY
12. HELP
13. GERMANY
    PERSECUTED
    ANABAPTISTS
14. MICHAEL SERVETUS
15. STUDY
16. FALSE DOCTRINE
17. RE-BAPTIZER
18. WALDENSES
    LOLLARDS
    ALBIGENSES
    WELSH
    BAPTISTS
19. WILLIAM TYNDALE
    WELSH BAPTIST
20. RACK
    ANABAPTIST CATCHER

Lesson Twelve
1. IDENTIFYING TOOL
2. THIRTEENTH
   FIFTEENTH
3. REBAPTIZE
4. HISTORY
5. ONE
   LOCAL CHURCH

Answer Key

6. CHILD OF GOD
7. MODE
8. IMMERSION INTO WATER
9. MODES
10. DEATH
    BURIAL
    RESURRECTION
11. GOSPEL
12. BAPTISTS
13. GREBEL
    FATHER
    ANABAPTISTS
14. BLAUROCK
    THOUSANDS
15. GEORGE BLAUROCK
    1529
16. BALTHASER HUBMAIER
17. 6,000
18. FELIX MANS
19. MICHAEL SATTLER
20. MENNO SIMONS
21. GREAT
22. EVERYONE
23. BLOODY